Ancient Paths

Ancient Paths

Matthew Petchinsky

Ancient Paths: The 13 Sacred Principles of Dino Wicca
By: Matthew Petchinsky

Stepping into the Prehistoric Sacred

Throughout human history, people have sought deeper connections with nature, the spirits of the land, and the wisdom of ancient beings. From the druids who revered sacred groves to the shamans who communed with the spirits of animals, our ancestors understood that power resides in the past, in the bones of the earth, and in the echoes of those who came before us. Dino Wicca is the next evolution of that understanding—a spiritual path that weaves together the energies of prehistoric creatures with the timeless principles of magick and reverence for the natural world.

Dino Wicca is not a reconstructionist tradition, nor is it a mere fascination with dinosaurs. It is a living, breathing magickal path that honors the primal energies of Earth's most ancient and powerful inhabitants—the dinosaurs. These colossal beings ruled the planet for millions of years, embodying resilience, strength, adaptability, and transformation. Their spirits, fossilized in stone and embedded in the very fabric of the earth, continue to hold great power for those who seek their guidance.

At the heart of Dino Wicca lies a sacred framework: **The 13 Sacred Principles**—a set of guiding tenets that serve as the foundation for this unique path. These principles act as a spiritual compass, helping practitioners align with the essence of prehistoric wisdom, deepening their magickal practices, and fostering a sense of harmony between themselves and the ancient forces that still whisper through time.

The 13 Sacred Principles: The Spiritual Foundation of Dino Wicca

The **13 Sacred Principles of Dino Wicca** serve as both a moral and mystical code, shaping how practitioners interact with the energies of the universe, the spirits of prehistoric creatures, and the rhythms of nature itself. Each principle embodies a lesson drawn from the prehistoric past—teachings of endurance, survival, balance, and reverence for the world around us. These principles are not rigid rules but living truths, meant to be understood, internalized, and applied in a way that resonates with each individual's journey.

By following these principles, Dino Wiccans create a sacred bond with the primal forces that existed long before human civilization and will continue to exist long after. The goal is not to worship dinosaurs as deities, but to channel their wisdom and strength into personal growth, spiritual practice, and magickal workings.

The Importance of the 13 Sacred Principles in Everyday Life and Magickal Practice

Living in harmony with these sacred principles does not mean retreating into an archaic way of life; rather, it means integrating the lessons of the past into the present. The energy of the Stegosaurus teaches patience and stability, the ferocity of the Tyrannosaurus rex reminds us to stand strong in our power, and the adaptability of the Velociraptor urges us to move with intelligence and cunning in the face of change.

In magickal practice, these principles form the cornerstone of spellwork, rituals, and spiritual connection. Whether one is crafting spells for protection, calling upon the spirit of the Triceratops for guidance in overcoming obstacles, or seeking the wisdom of the Pterosaurs for insight and higher knowledge, these principles ensure that every act of magick is performed in alignment with ancient energies that transcend time.

Understanding and applying the **13 Sacred Principles** allows practitioners to walk a path that is not only magickal but also deeply transformative. It fosters an awareness of the interconnectedness between all living beings—past, present, and future. By aligning with these ancient forces, Dino Wiccans embrace the ever-evolving dance of existence, just as the dinosaurs once did, adapting, thriving, and leaving behind their sacred imprint upon the Earth.

Setting Intentions for Harmony with the Dino Wiccan Path

As we embark on this journey into **Ancient Paths: The 13 Sacred Principles of Dino Wicca**, it is important to begin with **clear intentions**. Setting intentions allows us to open ourselves fully to the teachings ahead, ensuring that we absorb these principles with sincerity and a willingness to grow.

Before diving into the sacred principles, take a moment to center yourself. Reflect on why you have been drawn to this path. Are you seeking deeper spiritual connection? A new way to approach magick? A means to balance your inner world with the ancient forces of nature? Whatever your reason, let it be your guiding light as you move forward.

Consider lighting a candle, holding a fossil or crystal associated with ancient energies, and speaking an invocation to welcome the wisdom of prehistoric spirits into your practice. An example of an intention-setting affirmation might be:

"I step upon the sacred ground of the ancient past,
With open heart and willing spirit.
May the wisdom of the prehistoric world guide me,
May the strength of the great beasts empower me,
May the 13 Sacred Principles shape my journey,
As I walk in harmony with the echoes of time."

With this intention in place, you are ready to explore the **13 Sacred Principles of Dino Wicca**—principles that will transform not only your spiritual practice but also the way you move through the world.

Let us step forward, into the prehistoric sacred.

Chapter 1: The Principle of Acceptance of All

The first of the **13 Sacred Principles of Dino Wicca** is the **Principle of Acceptance of All**—a foundational tenet that promotes inclusivity, harmony, and an open heart toward the diversity of life, both past and present. This principle is rooted in the prehistoric past, where countless species coexisted, each fulfilling a vital role in the intricate web of existence.

In Dino Wicca, the energy of acceptance mirrors the way Earth sustained a vast variety of beings, from towering Brachiosaurs to swift Velociraptors, from the smallest insects to the mighty apex predators. Each played its part in maintaining the balance of prehistoric ecosystems. Likewise, in modern spiritual practice, accepting others regardless of differences—be they cultural, spiritual, physical, or personal—is essential in creating a community of mutual respect and growth.

Embracing Diversity within Dino Wicca

Dino Wicca is a **path of inclusion**, welcoming practitioners from all backgrounds, identities, and walks of life. Just as the vast landscapes of prehistory supported countless species, Dino Wicca encourages the recognition that diversity is a strength, not a division.

Acceptance within Dino Wicca extends to multiple aspects of existence:

1. **Accepting Different Spiritual Paths** – Some practitioners may incorporate elements of other traditions, while others follow Dino Wicca exclusively. There is no "one true way," only the path that resonates with the individual.
2. **Respecting Personal Identities** – Just as the prehistoric world was filled with creatures of all sizes, forms, and adaptations, humanity, too, is diverse in gender, sexuality, abilities, and cultural heritage. Dino Wicca embraces and celebrates these differences.
3. **Honoring All Creatures** – Dino Wicca teaches that every being, from the tiniest microorganism to the mightiest dinosaur, held its own sacred place in the world. This perspective reminds practitioners to honor all life—human, animal, spiritual, and beyond.

By embracing acceptance in all its forms, Dino Wiccans create a spiritual practice that is not only meaningful to themselves but also welcoming to others.

How Acceptance Fosters Unity in Both Spiritual and Mundane Realms

In both the **spiritual** and **mundane** aspects of life, the Principle of Acceptance plays a vital role in fostering unity.

- **Spiritual Acceptance**: When practitioners accept and embrace differing viewpoints, beliefs, and magickal practices, they create an environment of shared wisdom. Rather than seeing differences as obstacles, they become opportunities to learn and grow.
- **Mundane Acceptance**: In everyday life, practicing acceptance helps dissolve barriers between people. It allows individuals to interact with kindness, build stronger communities, and overcome prejudice. It also extends to self-acceptance, which is a crucial step in any spiritual journey.

Unity does not mean sameness; rather, it means recognizing that each person, like each prehistoric species, has something valuable to contribute. A world where only one type of dinosaur existed would have been unsustainable—diversity ensured survival. The same holds true for spiritual communities. By accepting and valuing differences, we build a collective strength that empowers all members.

Rituals for Self-Acceptance and Community Inclusivity

The Principle of Acceptance begins within. Before we can fully accept others, we must first embrace ourselves—our flaws, strengths, past mistakes, and future potential. Below are two powerful rituals to cultivate **self-acceptance** and **community inclusivity** within Dino Wicca.

Ritual for Self-Acceptance: The Fossil Reflection Ceremony

Purpose: This ritual helps practitioners recognize their own worth and embrace self-love, much like how the Earth preserves fossils—each unique, valuable, and a part of the grand design.

Materials:

- A fossil (real or symbolic, such as a stone or shell)
- A mirror
- A candle (any color that represents self-acceptance to you)
- A bowl of salt water

Steps:

1. **Prepare Your Space**: Find a quiet place where you will not be disturbed. Light the candle and place the mirror in front of you. Hold the fossil or stone in your hands.
2. **Reflection and Release**: Look into the mirror and say aloud:

"As this fossil is shaped by time, so too am I. My past has shaped me, but it does not define me. I accept myself fully, as I am and as I am becoming."

1. **Cleansing and Renewal**: Dip your fingers into the salt water and touch your forehead, heart, and hands, symbolizing the cleansing of self-doubt and the renewal of self-acceptance.
2. **Closing**: Hold the fossil close to your heart and say:

"Like the bones of the ancients, my spirit is strong. Like the wisdom of the past, my worth is undeniable. I honor my path, my presence, and my power."

1. **Extinguish the Candle**: Let the candle burn safely for a few minutes as you meditate on the ritual's meaning. Then, snuff it out, thanking the energies you invoked.

Repeat this ritual whenever you feel the need to reconnect with self-love and acceptance.

Community Inclusivity Ritual: The Circle of the Prehistoric Sacred

Purpose: This group ritual fosters inclusivity and unity among Dino Wiccans, allowing practitioners to symbolically and spiritually accept one another into the sacred path.

Materials:

- A circle of stones or wooden dinosaur carvings
- A central candle (white for unity, green for growth, or red for strength)
- A feather, fossil, or other sacred token to pass around

Steps:

1. **Form a Circle**: Gather in a sacred space and place the stones or carvings in a circle around the candle. Each participant should hold hands or sit close together.
2. **Calling the Prehistoric Ancestors**: One person (or the group collectively) speaks:

"From the bones of the Earth to the spirits of the past, we honor the sacred wisdom of the prehistoric world. May we learn, may we grow, may we accept all as they are."

1. **The Passing of the Token**: Each person takes turns holding the fossil, feather, or sacred token and sharing a short phrase about what acceptance means to them. (Example: "I accept all paths, for all paths lead to wisdom.")
2. **Unity Chant**: Once the token has been passed around, the group recites together:

"Like the great herds that roamed the ancient plains, we stand together. Like the mighty rivers that carved the land, we flow as one. We are Dino Wicca. We are strong in our unity."

1. **Closing the Ritual**: The candle is extinguished, and participants thank the spirits of the prehistoric world before departing.

This ritual can be performed whenever a new member joins the community or when a group seeks to strengthen its bonds.

Conclusion: Walking the Path of Acceptance

The Principle of Acceptance of All is not just a spiritual ideal—it is a way of life. It teaches us to honor diversity, embrace ourselves, and extend inclusivity to others. By weaving this principle into our daily actions and magickal practices, we create a path that is as strong and enduring as the bones of the ancients.

Just as the Earth never rejected a creature for being different, Dino Wicca reminds us that all beings have a place in the sacred web of existence. By practicing **acceptance**, we step closer to the true essence of this path—one of unity, understanding, and reverence for all that was, is, and will be.

Chapter 2: The Principle of Respect for All Living Things

Respect is the foundation of all sacred relationships—between individuals, between species, and between the past, present, and future. In **Dino Wicca**, the **Principle of Respect for All Living Things** is a core tenet that acknowledges the intrinsic value of all forms of life, from the tiniest insect to the mightiest prehistoric beasts that once roamed the Earth.

This principle teaches that all beings—human, animal, plant, and spirit—are part of the **great web of existence**, interconnected in ways that are both seen and unseen. Respecting life means acknowledging that every creature has its purpose, its unique energy, and its role in the cosmic balance. To live by this principle is to honor the sacred essence of life, both in its present form and in the echoes of those who came before us.

Honoring the Sanctity of Life, from the Smallest Insect to the Mighty Dinosaur Spirit

The **dinosaurs** that once ruled the Earth existed in a vast, diverse ecosystem. From the tiny Microraptor flitting between branches to the towering Argentinosaurus that shook the ground with its steps, all beings played their part. Similarly, in modern times, we must recognize that every living thing contributes to the balance of the world, whether we understand its role or not.

Honoring life means:

1. **Recognizing the Value of Every Creature**
    - Just as no species was insignificant in prehistoric times, no creature today is without its purpose. Even insects, which many see as pests, are crucial for pollination, decomposition, and ecological balance.
    - In Dino Wicca, all creatures are seen as **spiritual teachers**. The spider teaches patience, the hawk teaches vision, and the great dinosaurs remind us of endurance and change.
2. **Respecting the Spirits of Prehistoric Beings**
    - Though dinosaurs are long extinct in the physical world, their spirits live on in the **energetic memory of the Earth**. Fossils are not just remnants of the past—they hold the echoes of ancient beings.
    - Honoring dinosaur spirits can be done through rituals, offerings, and meditations that invite their wisdom into your practice.
3. **Practicing Non-Harm Whenever Possible**
    - Just as the **herbivorous dinosaurs** lived in harmony with their world, so too should Dino Wiccans strive for harmony. Avoid harming animals unnecessarily, and show reverence for the environment that supports life.
    - While it is not always possible to avoid harm completely, the intent should always be to minimize suffering and act with kindness.
4. **Understanding the Circle of Life**
    - In nature, death is not an end but a transformation. Even the most powerful dinosaurs eventually returned to the Earth, feeding the cycle of renewal.
    - Respecting life also means respecting death as a necessary part of existence. This can be honored through ancestor work, rituals of remembrance, and ethical practices that show gratitude for life's gifts.

Daily Practices to Show Respect for Nature and Living Beings

Living by the **Principle of Respect for All Living Things** is not confined to ritual or sacred space—it is a **daily practice** that becomes part of the Dino Wiccan lifestyle. Here are simple yet powerful ways to cultivate this respect:

1. Speak and Act with Kindness

- Every word and action carries energy. Speaking kindly to people, animals, and even plants fosters harmony and balance.
- When working with herbs or crystals, thank them for their help. When using tools in magick, acknowledge their energies.

2. Offerings to the Earth and Animal Spirits

- Leave natural offerings such as **seeds, water, or biodegradable materials** to honor the spirits of the land.
- Dedicate a **small altar** to extinct creatures, placing fossils, feathers, or stones as a sign of remembrance.

3. Reduce Harmful Impact on Nature

- Limit waste, reduce plastic use, and practice sustainable living. Even small efforts, such as using reusable bags or recycling, demonstrate respect for the Earth.
- Choose eco-friendly rituals—avoid using non-biodegradable items in spellwork and be mindful of the materials in your magickal tools.

4. Honor the Animals in Your Daily Life

- Treat pets and wildlife with care. A simple act of feeding birds, helping an injured animal, or supporting conservation efforts aligns with the principle of respect.
- If you eat meat, do so **mindfully**, giving thanks to the animal that provided nourishment.

5. Sacred Listening to Nature

- Take time each day to **listen to the world around you**. Whether it's the rustling of leaves, the sound of birds, or the hum of insects, being present with nature strengthens the bond between you and the natural world.

Meditations to Deepen Your Connection with All Life

Meditation is a powerful way to cultivate **respect for all living things** by attuning yourself to the energies of nature and prehistoric spirits. Below are two guided meditations to help you deepen this connection.

Meditation 1: The Breath of the Ancient Beasts

Purpose: To align yourself with the spirit of prehistoric creatures and develop a sense of kinship with all life.

Steps:

1. Find a quiet space outdoors or near a plant. Sit comfortably and close your eyes.
2. Take deep, slow breaths, imagining the air filling your lungs as it did for the great dinosaurs millions of years ago.
3. Visualize yourself standing in a prehistoric landscape. Feel the ground beneath you, rich with the ancient energy of those who walked before.
4. See a dinosaur of your choice approach you. It may be a powerful T. rex, a wise Triceratops, or a gentle Apatosaurus.
5. Ask this being to share its wisdom. What does it teach you about respect? About the balance of life?
6. Listen to the message. When ready, thank the spirit and slowly bring your awareness back to the present moment.
7. Reflect on how you can apply its teachings to your daily life.

Meditation 2: The Web of Life Connection

Purpose: To experience the interconnectedness of all living things, strengthening your respect for the sacredness of life.

Steps:

1. Sit or lie down in a comfortable position. Close your eyes and focus on your breathing.
2. Visualize roots extending from your body into the Earth, connecting you to all living things.
3. Imagine a golden thread of energy linking you to every creature—birds, insects, mammals, plants, and even prehistoric spirits.
4. Feel their presence and recognize that you are a part of this vast web.
5. Silently offer gratitude to all forms of life. Send love and respect through the web, letting it flow to every being connected to you.
6. Slowly bring your awareness back, feeling renewed and deeply connected to the sacredness of all life.

Conclusion: Walking with the Ancient Ones in Harmony

The **Principle of Respect for All Living Things** is a sacred commitment to honoring life in all its forms. It reminds us that, just as the dinosaurs lived in balance with their world, we too must strive for harmony with nature, animals, and each other.

By practicing daily acts of respect, engaging in mindful rituals, and deepening our connection through meditation, we strengthen our relationship with the world and the ancient spirits that still linger within it.

As Dino Wiccans, we walk not alone but alongside the **echoes of the past**, the living beings of the present, and the future yet to come. By embodying respect, we ensure that our path remains one of wisdom, balance, and reverence for the sacred web of life.

May we honor all that walks, flies, swims, and once roamed this Earth. For in respect, we find unity. In unity, we find strength.

Chapter 3: The Principle of Connection to Prehistoric Wisdom

Throughout time, humans have sought guidance from their ancestors—whether human, animal, or spiritual. The **Principle of Connection to Prehistoric Wisdom** in Dino Wicca extends this idea beyond recorded history, reaching deep into the ancient past to commune with the spirits of the **dinosaurs and other prehistoric beings**.

The Earth has preserved the echoes of the past in fossils, stones, and energy imprints, waiting for those who are willing to listen. These ancient beings left behind not only their physical remains but also their **wisdom, instincts, and energy**, which can be tapped into for **guidance, protection, strength, and spiritual insight**.

Dino Wiccans believe that dinosaurs, like all creatures of nature, carried unique spiritual frequencies. By learning to **connect with prehistoric wisdom**, practitioners open themselves to an unbroken chain of **ancestral energy**—a lineage not of human blood, but of Earth's primal forces.

Tapping into the Ancestral Knowledge of Dinosaurs

Dinosaurs existed for over **165 million years**, adapting to changes, thriving in their ecosystems, and developing a **deep relationship with the Earth's energies**. Their spirits hold valuable lessons in survival, transformation, and resilience.

Ways to Access Prehistoric Wisdom
1. Fossil Meditation and Energy Reading

Fossils are **sacred relics** of prehistoric times, containing **energetic imprints** of the creatures they once were. By meditating with fossils, you can tap into their knowledge and align your energy with the **strength, endurance, and instincts** of the dinosaur spirit they represent.

How to Perform a Fossil Meditation:

- Find a **fossil**, preferably one that you feel drawn to. If you don't have a fossil, you can use a **stone from a prehistoric site** or even a **symbolic representation of a dinosaur**.
- Sit in a quiet space and hold the fossil in your hands.
- Close your eyes and take deep breaths, visualizing yourself in **a prehistoric world**.
- Imagine **the spirit of the dinosaur** emerging from the fossil, standing before you.
- Ask for its wisdom:

"Ancient one, guardian of forgotten ages, grant me the knowledge you carry. Teach me the lessons of endurance, strength, and balance."

- Listen to any messages, sensations, or visions you receive.
- When finished, thank the spirit and journal your experience.

2. Dreamwork and Dino Spirit Visitations

Dinosaurs often appear in dreams as guides, warning spirits, or messengers. If you wish to receive direct wisdom from them, setting an intention before sleep can invite their presence.

Prehistoric Dream Invocation:

- Before bed, place a **fossil, stone, or dinosaur figurine** under your pillow or near your bed.
- Say a simple invocation:

"May the wisdom of the great beasts enter my dreams,
May the ancient ones walk with me tonight,
May I awaken with knowledge of the past."

- Keep a **dream journal** to record any visions, messages, or interactions with dinosaur spirits.

3. Nature Immersion and Earth Connection

Dinosaurs were deeply in tune with the Earth's cycles, landscapes, and ecosystems. To access their wisdom, spend time in **natural settings**—forests, mountains, rivers, or even fossil sites—where the energy of prehistoric life still lingers.

- **Walk barefoot** to ground yourself to the land.
- Sit in silence and ask, **"What can the Earth teach me today?"**
- Observe **patterns in nature**, as they often hold clues to ancient knowledge.

Exploring Fossil Magick and Prehistoric Symbols

Fossils are not just remnants of the past; they are **powerful tools for magick and energy work**. Dino Wiccans use fossils in rituals for **protection, transformation, and ancestral connection**.

Using Fossils in Magick

1. **Fossil Protection Amulet**
    - Carry a fossil in your **pocket, bag, or altar** to shield yourself from negative energy.
    - Infuse it with intent by chanting:

"Bone of the past, guard my path,
Ancient shield, keep me safe at last."

1. **Fossil Charging for Strength**
    - Hold a fossil and visualize **drawing strength** from the ancient energy within it.
    - This is especially useful during difficult times or when facing challenges.
2. **Fossil Scrying for Prehistoric Guidance**
    - Fill a bowl with **water** and place a fossil inside.
    - Gaze into the water and allow **visions or messages** to emerge.

Prehistoric Symbols in Dino Wicca

Just as ancient cultures had sacred symbols, Dino Wiccans use **prehistoric imagery** in magickal work:

- **Triceratops Horns** – Symbolize **protection and endurance**.
- **Tyrannosaurus Claw** – Represents **power and primal energy**.
- **Pterosaur Wings** – Signify **freedom and higher knowledge**.
- **Fossil Spiral (Ammonite)** – A symbol of **evolution and cosmic cycles**.

These symbols can be **carved into candles, worn as charms, or drawn in ritual circles** to invoke their energy.

Techniques for Invoking Dino Spirits in Your Rituals

Dino spirits can be powerful allies in **ritual work, spellcasting, and divination**. Below are techniques to call upon them.

1. Calling the Prehistoric Guardians

Before any major ritual, invoke **the spirits of the ancient world** to lend their power.

Invocation Example:

"Spirits of the primordial past,
Beasts of bone and time so vast,
Walk with me in sacred space,
Guide my heart with ancient grace."

As you speak, visualize **a dinosaur spirit** appearing, circling you, and **charging your ritual with energy**.

2. Dino Spirit Candle Magick

Choose a **candle color** that aligns with your intention:

- **Red (Strength, Protection)** – T. rex Energy
- **Green (Growth, Balance)** – Brachiosaurus Wisdom
- **Blue (Spiritual Connection)** – Pterosaur Insight

Carve a **prehistoric symbol** into the candle, light it, and focus on **drawing power from the ancient spirits**.

3. Guided Journey to the Prehistoric Realm

If you wish to meet your **dinosaur spirit guide**, try this visualization:

1. Sit in meditation, breathing deeply.
2. Imagine yourself walking **through a misty jungle**.
3. As the mist clears, see **a dinosaur approaching you**.
4. Observe its form, size, and movements—what wisdom does it carry?
5. Ask for its guidance.
6. When ready, thank the spirit and **slowly return to the present moment**.

This **shamanic-style journey** can provide **deep insights** into your spiritual path.

Conclusion: Walking with the Ancients

The **Principle of Connection to Prehistoric Wisdom** is an invitation to **embrace the echoes of the past**, learning from beings who ruled the Earth long before humans walked its surface.

By **honoring fossils, working with prehistoric symbols, and invoking dinosaur spirits**, Dino Wiccans create a **bridge between past and present**, allowing **ancient knowledge to guide their modern lives**.

The great beasts may no longer roam the land, but their energy endures. By aligning with their wisdom, we **stand stronger, think deeper, and walk with the power of ages past**.

May the **spirits of the ancient world** walk with you, always.

Chapter 4: The Principle of Evolution and Personal Growth

Evolution is the force that shapes all life. It is a **sacred dance of transformation**, one that has played out for billions of years, guiding species through changes, challenges, and adaptations. In **Dino Wicca**, the **Principle of Evolution and Personal Growth** serves as a reminder that we, like the dinosaurs before us, are on an ever-changing journey.

Dinosaurs were not static beings. Over **165 million years**, they evolved into countless species—some growing larger, some adapting to new environments, and some even evolving into the birds we see today. Their ability to change ensured their survival across the ages. This same principle applies to us. **Personal growth, transformation, and self-discovery are part of the sacred path**.

To honor this principle, Dino Wiccans commit to **continual learning, self-improvement, and embracing change rather than fearing it**. By aligning with the wisdom of the ancient world, we understand that we are not meant to remain stagnant—we are meant to evolve, grow, and thrive.

Understanding Life as a Continuous Journey of Transformation

Change is inevitable. Just as species adapt or fade away, humans must **evolve spiritually, emotionally, and intellectually**. The **mistake many make is resisting transformation**, fearing the unknown instead of embracing the lessons it brings.

Three Truths About Evolution and Growth

1. **Nothing is Permanent—And That's a Good Thing**
   - The world is in constant motion, and so are we. Every stage of life brings **new challenges, new wisdom, and new forms of self-discovery**.
   - Instead of fearing change, Dino Wiccans learn to **flow with it**, using it as a tool for transformation.
2. **Growth Requires Adaptation**
   - Dinosaurs thrived because they **adapted to their environments**. Those that could not change eventually disappeared.
   - In personal growth, we must also be willing to **shed old habits, perspectives, and limitations** that no longer serve us.
3. **Setbacks Are Part of the Journey**
   - Not every dinosaur survived every extinction event—but those that did **grew stronger and evolved** into new forms.
   - Failure is **not the end**—it is part of the process. Every setback offers an opportunity for **learning and transformation**.

Ask Yourself:

- What is holding me back from evolving into my best self?
- What outdated beliefs or fears do I need to let go of?
- How can I align myself with my true potential?

By understanding that **life is a journey, not a destination**, we embrace evolution as part of our sacred path.

Lessons from the Adaptability of Dinosaurs Over Millennia

Dinosaurs **mastered survival** because of their adaptability. Their **strength was not just in size or power—it was in their ability to change.**

Key Lessons from Dinosaur Evolution

1. Adapt or Perish: The Lesson of the Avian Dinosaurs

Not all dinosaurs went extinct. Some **evolved into birds**, adapting to new conditions by developing feathers, lightweight bones, and flight.

What This Teaches Us:

- We must be **willing to change** when life demands it.
- Holding onto the past too tightly prevents **growth and transformation**.
- Sometimes, the best way to survive is to **evolve into something new**.

2. Strength Comes in Many Forms: The Lesson of the Triceratops

The Triceratops was not the biggest dinosaur, but it had **adaptations that made it powerful**—strong horns for defense, a thick frill for protection, and a keen ability to sense danger.

What This Teaches Us:

- Strength isn't always about being the most powerful—it's about using your abilities wisely.
- Personal growth isn't about **competing** with others but **harnessing your own unique strengths**.
- Protecting yourself while still **standing your ground** is a powerful skill.

3. Timing is Everything: The Lesson of the Velociraptor

Velociraptors were **small but highly intelligent predators**, using **strategy and timing** to hunt rather than brute force.

What This Teaches Us:

- Growth happens **when the time is right**—rushing things can lead to failure.
- Patience and planning **are key to success**.
- Intelligence and adaptability **often win over strength alone**.

By **applying these lessons to our own lives**, we learn to navigate **challenges, setbacks, and transformations with wisdom and confidence.**

Exercises to Foster Personal and Spiritual Growth

Now that we understand the importance of **evolution and adaptability**, let's explore exercises to actively cultivate **personal and spiritual growth**.

1. The Fossil Release Ritual: Letting Go of the Past

Purpose: This ritual helps release **old habits, fears, and thought patterns** that no longer serve you.

Materials:

- A small **fossil or stone** (to represent past burdens)
- A **bowl of water**
- A **black candle** (symbolizing transformation)

Steps:

1. Light the candle and hold the fossil in your hands.
2. Close your eyes and reflect on something **holding you back**—a fear, limiting belief, or bad habit.
3. Whisper your intention:

"As the past turns to stone, I release what no longer serves me. I evolve, I grow, I transform."

1. Place the fossil in the **bowl of water**, visualizing your burden **washing away**.
2. Snuff the candle and let the fossil dry, knowing you are free from what once held you back.

Repeat this ritual whenever you feel **stuck in old patterns**.

2. The Evolutionary Journal: Tracking Growth Over Time

Purpose: To track **personal progress** and recognize how much you have evolved.

How to Do It:

- Keep a **journal dedicated to your growth**.
- Every month, write down:
    - What lessons you have learned.
    - What challenges you overcame.
    - How you have changed from the previous month.
- After **six months**, look back and reflect:
    - What themes repeat?
    - Where have you evolved?
    - What areas still need growth?

This helps **recognize progress**, even when it feels slow.

3. Dinosaur Totem Visualization: Embodying Ancient Strength
Purpose: To channel **dinosaur energy** for personal empowerment.
Steps:

1. Close your eyes and take **deep breaths**.
2. Imagine yourself **in a prehistoric world**.
3. See a **dinosaur approaching you**—it is **your spirit guide**.
4. Observe:
     - What species is it?
     - What qualities does it embody? (Strength, speed, wisdom?)
     - What message does it bring?
5. Absorb its energy into your **own spirit**, feeling empowered by its presence.
6. When ready, **thank the dinosaur spirit** and return to the present.

Use this technique whenever you **need guidance or strength** in a difficult situation.

Conclusion: Embracing the Power of Change

The **Principle of Evolution and Personal Growth** reminds us that we are **always changing, always learning, always transforming**. The dinosaurs **did not resist change—they became it**. Some grew larger, some became faster, some evolved into entirely new beings.

By embracing this **ever-evolving nature**, Dino Wiccans step into their true power. We are not meant to be stagnant—we are meant to **shed old layers, adapt, and grow stronger**.

As you move forward, remember:

- Change is **not an enemy**—it is an ally.
- Growth is **not linear**—it happens in cycles.
- Transformation is **not a choice**—it is part of existence.

May you **walk the path of the ancients, evolve with wisdom, and grow into the powerful being you are destined to become**.

Chapter 5: The Principle of Harmony with the Earth

The Earth is our sacred home—a vast and ever-changing entity that has nurtured life for billions of years. It has witnessed the rise and fall of countless species, including the mighty dinosaurs, and it continues to sustain us today. In **Dino Wicca**, the **Principle of Harmony with the Earth** is one of the most fundamental teachings, reminding us that we must **live in balance with nature, honor the land, and act as responsible stewards of the environment.**

The dinosaurs thrived because they existed **within the natural cycles of the Earth**. They adapted to the landscapes, the climate shifts, and the resources available to them. In contrast, modern humanity has often disrupted these cycles, prioritizing convenience over sustainability. **Dino Wicca calls upon us to learn from the ancient world—to realign ourselves with the Earth's wisdom and respect the delicate balance that sustains all life.**

This chapter explores **ways to live in harmony with the Earth, guidance for sustainable living through Dino Wicca, and rituals to honor the planet's energies and cycles.**

Living in Balance with Nature and Respecting the Planet

To be in harmony with the Earth means to **respect it as a living entity**—not just as a resource to be used, but as a sacred being deserving of care and reverence.

1. Recognizing the Earth as a Living Being

- Many ancient cultures viewed the Earth as a sentient force, often referred to as **Gaia, the Great Mother, or the World Spirit.**
- In Dino Wicca, we see the Earth as a **guardian of ancient wisdom**, a force that has shaped and nurtured life for millions of years.
- By treating the Earth as a conscious entity, we foster a **deep spiritual connection** and cultivate gratitude for the land we walk upon.

2. Understanding the Earth's Cycles and Our Place Within Them

The Earth operates in **cycles**—the turning of the seasons, the rise and fall of ecosystems, the shifting of the land itself. Just as the dinosaurs **lived in sync with these cycles**, so too must we.

- **Seasonal Shifts**: Just as different dinosaurs thrived in different climates and time periods, we must **adjust our lifestyles to align with nature's rhythms.**
- **The Cycle of Life and Death**: Nothing in nature is wasted; all things **return to the Earth**. By embracing this truth, we learn to live more sustainably.
- **Planetary Changes**: The Earth is constantly evolving, and we must **respect its transformations rather than resist them.**

3. Adopting a Mindful Relationship with the Natural World

Being in harmony with the Earth means **listening to what it needs**. This can be done through:

- **Observing nature**: Noticing shifts in weather, animal behavior, and plant growth.
- **Spending time outdoors**: Walking, grounding (barefoot on the earth), and meditating in natural spaces.
- **Giving back**: Planting trees, cleaning up natural spaces, and reducing waste.

By developing a **conscious, reciprocal relationship** with the planet, we embody the true essence of harmony.

Dino Wicca's Guidance for Sustainable Living and Environmental Stewardship

The dinosaurs lived in **balance with their ecosystems**, never taking more than they needed. **Dino Wicca teaches us to follow this example through mindful, sustainable living.**

1. Reduce Your Ecological Footprint

To live in harmony with the Earth, **reduce your impact** by practicing:

- **Minimalism**: Avoid overconsumption—only take what you truly need.
- **Waste Reduction**: Reuse materials, recycle, and compost whenever possible.
- **Energy Conservation**: Use less electricity and water; opt for renewable energy sources.
- **Eco-Friendly Rituals**: Avoid plastic-based candles, synthetic incense, and non-biodegradable offerings.

2. Embracing Earth-Based Diets and Ethical Consumption

- **Eating sustainably**: Support local farmers, reduce food waste, and consume in alignment with the seasons.
- **Mindful consumption**: Choose products with **sustainable packaging** and ethical sourcing.
- **Respecting all life**: If you eat meat, honor the spirit of the animal by offering thanks.

3. Protecting the Land and Wildlife

- Support conservation efforts for **endangered species and natural habitats.**
- Avoid littering and damaging natural landscapes.
- Plant native plants to help restore ecosystems.

The Earth gave rise to **millions of species before us**, and it is our duty to ensure that it **continues to flourish for generations to come.**

Rituals to Honor the Earth's Cycles and Energies

Rituals help strengthen our bond with the Earth, attuning us to its rhythms and allowing us to express **gratitude and reverence**.

1. The Earth Connection Ritual

Purpose: To realign with the Earth's energy and ground oneself in harmony.

Materials:

- A **stone or fossil** (to represent Earth's ancient memory)
- A **bowl of soil**
- A **green or brown candle**

Steps:

1. Sit outdoors or near an open window.
2. Place your hands in the soil, feeling the **energy of the Earth beneath you.**
3. Hold the fossil or stone and close your eyes.
4. Breathe deeply and say:

"From the bones of the Earth, I was formed.
From the breath of the wind, I am sustained.
From the waters of time, I am renewed.
May I walk in harmony with the land."

1. Light the candle and meditate on how you can **live more in balance with nature.**
2. Extinguish the candle and **bury the soil outdoors as an offering.**

2. The Seasonal Honoring Ritual
Purpose: To celebrate the turning of the seasons and align with nature's cycles.
Materials:

- Seasonal elements (flowers, leaves, pinecones, shells)
- A bowl of **water**
- A **white candle**

Steps:

1. Create an **altar using natural materials** that represent the current season.
2. Light the candle and hold the bowl of water, reflecting on the **seasonal changes occurring around you**.
3. Say:

"As the Earth turns, so do I.
With each season, I grow and change.
I honor the cycle of life, the wisdom of the land,
And the spirits of the ancient past."

1. Sprinkle the water onto the ground as a **blessing for the Earth**.
2. Keep the **altar active** throughout the season, changing it as nature shifts.

3. The Fossil Offering Ritual
Purpose: To **pay homage to prehistoric ancestors and Earth's enduring wisdom**.
Materials:

- A **small fossil or stone**
- A **natural outdoor space**
- A handful of **seeds or grains**

Steps:

1. Hold the fossil and close your eyes, envisioning the **prehistoric world**.
2. Say a prayer to the ancient spirits:

"To the ones who came before,
To the land that shaped them,
To the wisdom that endures,
I offer my thanks."

1. Place the fossil on the ground and **scatter the seeds or grains** as an offering.
2. Leave the area **undisturbed**, knowing your gratitude has been received.

Conclusion: Becoming Guardians of the Earth

The **Principle of Harmony with the Earth** calls upon us to become **caretakers of the land**, just as the Earth once nurtured the great dinosaurs.

By living **sustainably, honoring the Earth's cycles, and practicing mindful stewardship**, we ensure that the **wisdom of the ancient past continues to guide the future**.

May we walk **in balance with nature**, learn from the rhythms of the Earth, and stand as **guardians of the land, just as the dinosaurs once roamed it**.

For in protecting the Earth, we honor all who came before—and all who will come after.

Chapter 6: The Principle of Courage and Strength

Courage and strength are at the heart of all transformation. Throughout history, the most enduring beings have been those that embraced resilience, adapted to change, and stood firm in the face of challenges. In **Dino Wicca**, the **Principle of Courage and Strength** teaches us to **channel the mighty energy of the dinosaurs to overcome fear, face adversity, and cultivate our own inner power**.

The dinosaurs were some of the most **resilient creatures to ever walk the Earth**. They survived drastic climate shifts, battled predators, and adapted to the changing world. Their spirits remind us that true strength is not just **physical power**, but **mental fortitude, emotional endurance, and the will to evolve**.

As Dino Wiccans, we honor their energy by learning to **stand tall in the face of fear**, embrace the unknown, and recognize that **we, too, carry the same primal resilience within us**.

Drawing Inspiration from the Resilience of Dinosaurs

Dinosaurs lived for **millions of years** because of their ability to **adapt, fight, and survive**. Whether they were the **ferocious Tyrannosaurus rex**, the **intelligent Velociraptor**, or the **sturdy Triceratops**, each species had its own form of strength.

By studying their **unique qualities**, we can learn how to embody **courage, resilience, and power** in our own lives.

1. Strength of the Tyrannosaurus Rex: Confidence and Leadership

- The **T. rex** was a dominant force, using its **size, presence, and raw power** to command its environment.
- This energy teaches us to **step into leadership, embrace our power, and trust in our abilities**.
- Those who connect with the **T. rex spirit** can learn to:
    - Stand tall even in difficult times.
    - Speak their truth without fear.
    - Command respect in their personal and professional lives.

Invocation of the T. Rex Spirit:

"Tyrant King of ancient lands,
Teach me strength and where to stand.
In challenge great, in battle tight,
Grant me courage, fierce and bright."

2. Endurance of the Triceratops: Standing Strong in Adversity

- The **Triceratops** had an incredible defense system—its frill and horns provided protection while allowing it to hold its ground.
- This dinosaur teaches **stability, endurance, and the ability to remain steadfast against hardship.**
- Those who connect with the **Triceratops spirit** learn to:
  - Protect themselves emotionally and energetically.
  - Develop patience and resilience in tough times.
  - Face conflicts **without backing down**, but with wisdom and balance.

Affirmation of Endurance:
"I stand strong, I hold my space,
No fear, no doubt, I know my place."

3. Intelligence of the Velociraptor: Strategic Courage

- Velociraptors were **fast, intelligent, and worked in teams,** showing that **courage isn't just about brute strength—it's also about strategy, adaptability, and quick thinking.**
- Those who connect with the **Velociraptor spirit** learn to:
  - Use their **mind as their greatest weapon.**
  - Overcome fear through preparation and resourcefulness.
  - Face life's challenges with a **sharp, clear mind.**

Velociraptor Strategy Mantra:
"With swift feet and clever mind,
I seek, I solve, the path I find."

By learning from these **three examples**, we gain a **full picture of courage and strength**—confidence, endurance, and strategy.

Overcoming Fears and Facing Challenges with Bravery

Fear is a natural part of life. Even the strongest dinosaurs had to **face predators, competition, and environmental changes**. The key is not to eliminate fear, but to **learn how to move through it with courage**.

The Dino Wiccan Approach to Facing Fear

1. **Acknowledge It** – Pretending fear doesn't exist gives it more power. Accept that fear is a natural part of growth.
2. **Identify the Root Cause** – Is it fear of failure? Fear of judgment? Fear of the unknown? **Understanding fear makes it easier to confront.**
3. **Call Upon the Strength of the Dinosaurs** – Imagine yourself channeling the energy of **a powerful dinosaur**—whether it's the **bravery of a T. rex, the resilience of a Triceratops, or the cunning of a Velociraptor.**
4. **Take Small Steps Forward** – Growth doesn't happen overnight. **Each step forward weakens fear's grip.**
5. **Celebrate Your Strength** – Every time you **push through fear**, acknowledge your courage. This strengthens your **inner resilience**.

Spells and Affirmations to Build Inner Strength

Magick is a powerful tool for developing **courage, self-confidence, and resilience**. Below are rituals and affirmations designed to **tap into the prehistoric strength that exists within you**.

1. The Fossil Strength Spell

Purpose: To draw upon the ancient power of fossils to **enhance personal strength and resilience**.

Materials:

- A **fossil or stone** (to represent ancient power)
- A **red candle** (symbolizing courage)
- A **bowl of salt** (for grounding and protection)

Steps:

1. Place the fossil in front of you and light the candle.
2. Sprinkle salt in a **circle around the fossil**, creating a **sacred boundary of protection**.
3. Hold your hands over the fossil and say:

"Ancient bones, old and wise,
Grant me strength, clear my eyes.
Like the beasts of time before,
Make me fearless, strong, and sure."

1. Visualize **golden energy flowing from the fossil into you**, filling you with **the raw power of the dinosaurs**.
2. Let the candle burn safely for a few moments, then **extinguish it, sealing the energy within**.

Carry the fossil with you whenever you need **a boost of strength**.

2. The Roar of Power Affirmation Ritual
Purpose: To **speak courage into existence**, drawing upon the power of the dinosaur's roar.
Steps:

1. Stand tall with feet firmly on the ground.
2. Take a deep breath, **channeling your inner dinosaur**.
3. With force and confidence, say:

"I am fierce, I am strong!
I walk with ancient power long!
No fear can shake me, no doubt remain,
I rise in courage once again!"

1. If you feel bold, **let out a deep, powerful roar**—symbolizing the release of fear.
2. Repeat this whenever you need a **surge of confidence**.

3. The Triceratops Shield of Protection Spell
Purpose: To create an **energetic barrier** of **protection and resilience** against negativity.
Materials:

- A **black candle** (for protection)
- A **small stone** (representing Triceratops armor)
- A piece of **string or twine**

Steps:

1. Light the black candle and hold the stone in your hand.
2. Wrap the **string around the stone**, imagining it forming an **impenetrable shield** around you.
3. Say:

"Triceratops, steady and wise,
Let no harm my spirit rise.

Guard my heart, keep me strong,
Let no fear remain for long."

1. Keep the stone as a **protective charm**, carrying it when facing **difficult situations**.

Conclusion: Walking with Strength and Courage

The **Principle of Courage and Strength** teaches us that **we are far more powerful than we believe**. The dinosaurs **did not fear the storms, the shifting lands, or the great predators—they adapted, they endured, and they evolved**.

By embracing their energy, we, too, can **overcome obstacles, face our fears, and cultivate an unshakable inner power**.

May you **walk boldly**, may you **stand strong**, and may you **carry the spirit of the ancient beasts within you, always**.

Chapter 7: The Principle of Sacred Time and Space

Time is an eternal force, flowing like an ancient river through the fabric of existence. The **Principle of Sacred Time and Space** in **Dino Wicca** teaches that just as dinosaurs lived in harmony with the land, the sky, and the shifting cycles of the Earth, we too must recognize the sacredness of both **where we are** and **when we are**.

Sacred time and space are the foundation of any spiritual practice. They provide **structure, alignment, and connection to the great energies of the past, present, and future**. In Dino Wicca, we create **altars and sacred spaces** to anchor our spiritual energy, attune ourselves to the **ancient rhythm of time**, and mark **important milestones** with reverence.

By learning to harness **both time and space as sacred tools**, we step into deeper **magickal awareness** and walk the path of the ancient world **with clarity and power**.

Creating Dino Wiccan Altars and Sacred Spaces

An **altar** is more than just a physical setup—it is a **portal to spiritual energy**, a dedicated place where we connect with **the wisdom of the prehistoric world**.

Elements of a Dino Wiccan Altar

A **Dino Wiccan altar** can be as **elaborate or simple** as you like, but it should include elements that reflect the **ancient forces** you are working with. Below are suggested altar components:

1. Fossils and Stones (Connection to Prehistoric Energy)

- **Fossils** serve as **anchors to the past**, carrying the energy of the creatures that once lived.
- **Ammonites** symbolize **cosmic cycles**.
- **Dinosaur teeth or bones (replicas if necessary)** represent **strength and endurance**.
- **Crystals** such as **petrified wood, obsidian, or agate** help channel Earth's energy.

2. Candles and Fire Elements (Time and Energy)

- **Green candles** represent **growth and life**.
- **Brown candles** symbolize **Earth and stability**.
- **Black candles** connect to **ancestral energy and the wisdom of the extinct**.
- A small **volcanic rock or lava stone** reminds us of the **ever-changing Earth**.

3. Water Elements (Fluidity and Change)

- A **bowl of water** represents the **primordial oceans** where life began.
- Adding **sea salt** connects to the **ancient seas** that dinosaurs once roamed.

4. Earth and Plant Life (Grounding and Connection)

- **Soil, leaves, or dried herbs** honor the landscapes dinosaurs thrived in.
- **Cactus or ferns** are wonderful altar plants, as ferns date back to the **age of the dinosaurs**.

5. Symbols and Representations

- **Dinosaur figurines or artwork** representing the **spirit animals** of your practice.
- **A spiral symbol** to reflect the never-ending cycles of time.
- **Feathers, bones, or resin sculptures** to embody the transition of dinosaurs into modern birds.

Your **Dino Wiccan altar** should **reflect your unique connection to prehistoric energy**. It is a **living space**—change it as needed to honor different seasons, celestial events, or personal transformations.

Aligning with the Ancient Rhythm of Time and Celestial Events

Dinosaurs lived under the same **celestial rhythms** that govern our world today. They roamed beneath the light of the Moon, migrated with the changing seasons, and witnessed great cosmic shifts. **Dino Wicca honors these cycles**, recognizing that time is more than just hours on a clock—it is **a sacred flow of energy**.

The Prehistoric Cosmic Calendar

To align with ancient time, we observe:

- **The Sun and Moon Cycles** – Just as dinosaurs thrived under different climates and planetary movements, we, too, can work with the Sun and Moon's influence.
- **The Seasons** – Honoring the Earth's cycles allows us to **move with the natural world rather than against it**.
- **Celestial Events** – Meteor showers, eclipses, and planetary alignments are moments of **cosmic power**, reflecting the **same celestial forces that shaped prehistoric Earth**.

1. The Moon and Dino Wiccan Practice

The Moon played an essential role in prehistoric ecosystems—affecting tides, migration patterns, and possibly even **the behaviors of nocturnal dinosaurs**. In Dino Wicca, the **phases of the Moon** guide our magickal workings.

- **New Moon (Beginnings & Transformation)** – A time for **setting intentions** and beginning new spiritual practices.
- **Full Moon (Power & Manifestation)** – A time to **harness raw energy**, seek guidance from the **ancient ones**, and work on protection spells.
- **Waning Moon (Release & Reflection)** – Ideal for **letting go of old habits**, fears, or energies that no longer serve you.

Ritual for Connecting with the Prehistoric Moon:

1. Stand outside under the Moon's light.
2. Hold a **fossil or crystal** in your hands and say:

"Ancient sky, shining bright,
Guide me through this sacred night.
As the Moon did for those before,
Let its wisdom teach me more."

1. Close your eyes and **meditate on the Moon's energy**, feeling the **timeless connection between you and the ancient world**.

2. Solstices and Equinoxes in Dino Wicca

Dinosaurs experienced **seasonal changes**, and their survival often depended on adapting to them. We honor these **seasonal shifts** by aligning with **the Wheel of Time**:

- **Spring Equinox** – Celebrate renewal and rebirth, much like the time of **new hatchlings**.
- **Summer Solstice** – Acknowledge the **height of power and energy**, reflecting the **thriving age of dinosaurs**.
- **Autumn Equinox** – Give thanks for abundance, as the Earth **begins its transition**.
- **Winter Solstice** – Honor the stillness and lessons of the past, much like the **slow survival of creatures in prehistoric winters**.

By honoring these **natural shifts**, we attune ourselves to **the same cycles that guided prehistoric life**.

Practices for Marking Sacred Moments and Milestones

Throughout life, we experience **personal milestones**—moments of change, transformation, and renewal. Just as the **Earth evolved through different ages**, we, too, undergo **phases of growth**.

1. The Fossilization Ritual (Marking Life Transitions)

This ritual honors **a major personal transformation**, just as **fossils preserve the memory of past worlds**.

Materials:

- A **small stone or fossil**
- A **candle** (any color that represents change to you)
- A bowl of **earth or sand**

Steps:

1. Light the candle and hold the **stone or fossil** in your hands.
2. Reflect on what part of your life is **changing or evolving**.
3. Say:

"Time moves forward, I embrace its flow.
Like the fossils, my wisdom grows.
I honor the past, but walk anew,
In sacred time, I rise in truth."

1. Bury the **stone in the bowl of earth**, symbolizing **the transformation taking root**.
2. Leave it there until you **fully embrace your transition**, then retrieve it and keep it as a **symbol of your journey**.

2. The Ancient Time Meditation (Connecting with the Prehistoric Past)

This meditation allows you to **step beyond time** and seek wisdom from **the ancient world**.

1. Sit in a quiet place and close your eyes.
2. Breathe deeply, imagining the **landscapes of the prehistoric Earth**.
3. Visualize yourself walking through an **ancient jungle**, feeling the **pulse of time itself**.
4. Ask the spirits of the past:

"What knowledge do you carry? What lessons remain?"

1. Listen. The answer may come as a **feeling, image, or sudden inspiration**.
2. When ready, open your eyes and **journal your experience**.

Conclusion: Walking in Sacred Time and Space

To embrace the **Principle of Sacred Time and Space** is to **walk with the ancients, honor the present, and prepare for the future**. By creating **sacred spaces, aligning with cosmic cycles, and marking important milestones**, we step into **a deeper, more powerful way of being**.

Time is not our enemy—it is a force to be honored and embraced. The dinosaurs knew this, and now, so do we.

Chapter 8: The Principle of Magickal Co-Creation

Magick is not a solitary force—it is a partnership between **ourselves, the energies of the universe, and the spirits that dwell within it**. The **Principle of Magickal Co-Creation** in **Dino Wicca** teaches us that we are **not alone in our manifestations**; we work **alongside the spirits of ancient beings**, blending their **primal power** with our own desires to create **real change** in the world.

The dinosaurs were powerful, adaptable, and deeply attuned to the **Earth's rhythms**. Their spirits remain, embedded in **fossils, ancient landscapes, and the energy of time itself**. By forging a relationship with these spirits, **we awaken ancient forces to aid us in our magickal workings**, amplifying our power and ensuring our spells resonate with the strength of prehistoric wisdom.

This chapter explores how to **partner with Dino spirits**, conduct **rituals that merge prehistoric energy with modern intentions**, and practice **co-creative spells** that yield tangible results.

Partnering with Dino Spirits to Manifest Intentions

Dinosaurs, as **primordial forces of nature**, embody different **magickal attributes**. When calling upon their spirits, we must **understand their unique energies** and how they can **support our manifestations**.

1. Identifying Your Dino Spirit Ally

Just as animals serve as **spirit guides**, different dinosaurs align with specific **goals and desires**. By choosing the right **prehistoric ally**, we strengthen our manifestations.

Dinosaur Spirit	Magickal Attributes	Best for Manifesting
Tyrannosaurus Rex	Strength, power, dominance	Confidence, leadership, breaking through obstacles
Velociraptor	Intelligence, strategy, agility	Quick decision-making, mental clarity, adaptability
Triceratops	Protection, resilience, boundaries	Emotional healing, shielding, standing your ground
Brachiosaurus	Growth, patience, wisdom	Long-term goals, financial stability, deep knowledge
Pteranodon	Freedom, travel, higher wisdom	Expanding horizons, creativity, overcoming limits
Stegosaurus	Grounding, stability, connection to Earth	Deepening spiritual awareness, home protection
Ankylosaurus	Defense, security, self-preservation	Warding off negativity, creating safe spaces

Dinosaur Spirit	Magickal Attributes	Best for Manifesting
Spinosaurus	Duality, balance, adaptability	Handling major life transitions, emotional strength

How to Choose Your Dino Spirit:

- **Meditate on your goal.** What do you need help with?
- **Research dinosaurs**—one may naturally call to you.
- **Observe dream signs**—if a specific dinosaur appears in your dreams, it may be guiding you.
- **Use a fossil or carved representation** as a **symbol of your Dino ally** on your altar.

Once chosen, you will **co-create your magickal workings** with this ancient force.

Rituals to Blend Prehistoric Energy with Modern Desires

To co-create magick with **Dino spirits**, we must first **invite them into our sacred space**, allowing their **ancient power** to merge with our intentions.

1. Calling Upon Dino Spirits Ritual

Purpose: To invite a specific Dino spirit to aid in a manifestation.

Materials:

- A **fossil** or a **symbolic representation** of the dinosaur
- A **candle** that represents your goal (e.g., red for power, green for growth, blue for wisdom)
- A bowl of **earth** (for grounding)
- A **small piece of paper** with your intention written on it

Steps:

1. **Create a sacred space** where you will not be disturbed.
2. **Hold the fossil in your hands**, breathing deeply. Close your eyes and envision the **dinosaur's spirit forming in front of you**.
3. **Light the candle**, saying:

"Ancient one, great and wise,
From stone and time, let spirits rise.
Walk with me in sacred space,
Guide my hands, empower my place."

1. Place the **intention paper in the bowl of earth**, symbolizing the **planting of your desire into the energy of the past and present**.
2. **Visualize the Dino spirit lending its power** to your intention—see it infusing strength, protection, or speed as needed.
3. When you feel the energy has reached its peak, say:

"Together we create, together we rise,
With ancient strength, my will complies."

1. Let the candle burn safely for a while before snuffing it out. Keep the fossil or dinosaur symbol on your altar as a **reminder of the ongoing partnership**.

Examples of Co-Creative Spells and Their Results

Once a **Dino spirit is present**, we can **blend their energy with spellwork** to create **powerful, tangible results**. Below are three examples of **Dino Wiccan co-creative spells** and the changes they can manifest.

1. The Tyrannosaurus Roar: A Spell for Unshakable Confidence

Purpose: To **overcome self-doubt and reclaim personal power**.

Materials:

- A **Tyrannosaurus figurine or fossil**
- A **red candle**
- A **mirror**

Steps:

1. **Light the red candle** and place the **T. rex symbol before you**.
2. Stand before the **mirror**, looking yourself directly in the eyes.
3. Say aloud:

"As the T. rex ruled the land,
I command my space, I take my stand.
No fear, no doubt, I claim my right,
With ancient power, I rise in might!"

1. If possible, **roar loudly**—channeling the primal energy within you.
2. Blow out the candle, knowing you **carry the strength of the T. rex** within you.

Result: Over time, you'll notice yourself **becoming bolder, speaking with authority, and overcoming hesitation**.

2. The Raptor's Cunning: A Spell for Quick Thinking and Strategy

Purpose: To sharpen the **mind, wit, and ability to make swift decisions**.

Materials:

- A **Velociraptor symbol or feather**
- A **yellow candle** (for intelligence)
- A small piece of **quartz crystal**

Steps:

1. **Hold the crystal and feather**, visualizing the **sharp mind of the Velociraptor** entering you.
2. **Light the yellow candle** and say:

"Raptor fleet, fast and wise,
Clear my mind, unveil the lies.
May I think, may I see,
Swift decisions, sharp and free."

1. Carry the **quartz with you** for enhanced **mental clarity and focus**.

Result: You will find yourself **thinking faster, making better choices, and adapting to new situations with ease**.

3. The Stegosaurus Shield: A Spell for Protection and Boundaries

Purpose: To **create strong energetic and emotional protection**.

Materials:

- A **Stegosaurus symbol or stone**
- A **black candle**
- A bowl of **salt**

Steps:

1. **Create a circle of salt** around you, symbolizing protection.
2. **Light the black candle** and hold the **Stegosaurus symbol**, saying:

"Mighty beast, armored well,
Guard my space, cast your spell.
No harm shall pass, no ill remain,
Stegosaur spirit, my walls maintain."

1. Visualize an **energetic shield forming around you**, like the armored plates of a Stegosaurus.

Result: You will notice **less negativity around you**, feel **emotionally stronger**, and experience **fewer energy drains**.

Conclusion: Co-Creating Magick with the Ancient Ones

The **Principle of Magickal Co-Creation** teaches us that we are **not alone in our manifestations**. By partnering with **Dino spirits**, we amplify our power and ensure our desires are backed by **ancient, unbreakable strength**.

May you **walk beside the great beasts**, may your magick **rise like the tides of time**, and may your intentions **manifest with prehistoric force!**

Chapter 9: The Principle of Gratitude and Abundance

Gratitude is one of the most powerful forces in the universe. It is the foundation of **abundance, prosperity, and spiritual fulfillment**. In **Dino Wicca**, the **Principle of Gratitude and Abundance** teaches that **when we honor what we already have, we open the door for even greater blessings**.

The dinosaurs, despite their vast differences in size, shape, and survival methods, thrived in a world of **natural abundance**. The Earth provided them with food, shelter, and everything they needed to flourish. Even in times of great change—ice ages, shifting climates, and natural disasters—some species **adapted, survived, and continued to evolve. This is the key lesson of abundance: it is always present, but it requires gratitude and awareness to truly recognize it.**

By cultivating **a mindset of thankfulness, seeing abundance in all aspects of life, and performing ceremonies to express gratitude**, we align ourselves with the **flow of prosperity, ensuring that we receive what we need when we need it.**

Cultivating a Mindset of Thankfulness in Dino Wicca

Gratitude is more than just saying "thank you" when something good happens—it is a **spiritual practice** that transforms how we experience life. **When we live in gratitude, we shift from a mindset of scarcity to one of abundance.**

1. **The Power of Gratitude in Magick and Everyday Life**

- Gratitude **raises your vibration**, making it easier to attract **positive energy and opportunities**.
- It helps you **release fear and doubt**, as you begin to focus on what is already **working in your favor**.
- Gratitude creates a **stronger connection with the Earth, the Dino spirits, and the energy of time itself.**

2. **Gratitude as a Daily Spiritual Practice**

To fully embrace the **Principle of Gratitude and Abundance**, incorporate **small but powerful acts of gratitude** into your everyday life.

Dino Wiccan Gratitude Practices

◈ **Morning Fossil Blessing** – Hold a fossil or stone each morning and say:

"Ancient Earth, I honor you,
For all you've given, old and new.
I walk in gratitude today,
Let abundance light my way."

◈ **The Gratitude Jar** – Keep a **jar** or **bowl** where you place a note of **one thing you are thankful for every day**.

◈ **Thanking the Spirits of the Past** – Each night, offer a small **bowl of water or seeds outside,** saying:

"To those who walked before, I give my thanks.
May your wisdom guide me,
May my heart remain open,
And may abundance flow evermore."

◈ **Gratitude Walk** – Take **a walk in nature** and silently list everything you are grateful for—**the air, the land, the sky, the animals, and the spirits of prehistoric wisdom**.

By making **gratitude an intentional practice**, you **rewire your energy field to attract more of what you are thankful for**.

Recognizing Abundance in All Forms

Many people believe **abundance only refers to money**, but in reality, **abundance manifests in many different ways**. Dino Wiccans understand that prosperity comes in all forms:

Form of Abundance	Examples
Material Wealth	Money, resources, possessions
Natural Abundance	Clean water, fertile land, a thriving ecosystem
Knowledge & Wisdom	Learning, spiritual growth, ancestral guidance
Community & Support	Friendships, love, mentorship, opportunities
Health & Vitality	Energy, strength, longevity

Dinosaurs thrived in a world full of **natural abundance**—food sources, migration routes, and ecosystems that supported their survival. Some lived in **massive herds**, while others formed **symbiotic relationships** to share resources. **The key to abundance is recognizing that you are already surrounded by it.**

How to Shift from Scarcity to an Abundance Mindset

◈ **Scarcity Mindset**: "I don't have enough."
◈ **Abundance Mindset**: "The universe provides everything I need."
◈ **Scarcity Mindset**: "I need more money to be happy."
◈ **Abundance Mindset**: "I am rich in knowledge, love, and opportunity."
◈ **Scarcity Mindset**: "I'll never have the life I want."
◈ **Abundance Mindset**: "Every day, I attract the life I desire."

When you **train yourself to see abundance everywhere, more abundance flows into your life effortlessly**.

Ceremonies to Give Thanks and Attract Prosperity

Gratitude rituals are one of the **most powerful ways** to call abundance into your life. By **honoring what you already have**, you create an **energetic invitation for more to come**.

1. The Fossil of Gratitude Ceremony

Purpose: To express deep appreciation and open yourself to more blessings.

Materials:

- A **fossil, stone, or special object**
- A **green or gold candle** (symbolizing abundance)
- A **bowl of seeds or grains** (offering to nature)

Steps:

1. Light the candle and hold the fossil in your hands.
2. Close your eyes and **think of all the things you are grateful for**—big or small.
3. Say:

"Ancient Earth, old and wise,
I thank you now, I recognize.
For love, for strength, for all I gain,
May abundance flow again and again."

1. Place the **bowl of seeds outside** as an offering to the land and its spirits.

◈ **Result:** You will feel **lighter, more open, and attract new blessings** within days.

2. The Dino Prosperity Spell

Purpose: To call financial and material abundance into your life.

Materials:

- A **gold or green candle**
- A **Tyrannosaurus or Brachiosaurus figure or fossil**
- A **coin or bill**
- A **bowl of earth or sand**

Steps:

1. Light the candle and place the **fossil/dinosaur symbol in front of you**.
2. Hold the **coin or bill**, visualizing **financial abundance flowing into your life**.
3. Say:

"Mighty beast of ancient days,
Teach me how prosperity stays.
Like Earth provides, like waters flow,
May my wealth and blessings grow!"

1. Bury the coin in the **bowl of earth** overnight, then carry it with you for luck.

◈ **Result:** Expect **new financial opportunities, unexpected gifts, or career growth**.

3. The Gratitude Fire Ceremony

Purpose: To burn away limiting beliefs and make space for greater abundance.

Materials:

- A **fire-safe bowl or cauldron**
- A **small piece of paper**
- A **black and gold candle**

Steps:

1. Write down **any fears, doubts, or limiting beliefs** about money, love, or success.
2. Light the **black candle**, saying:

"I release the fears that block my way,
I step into abundance today."

1. Burn the paper in the **fire-safe bowl** and let the ashes return to the Earth.
2. Light the **gold candle**, saying:

"With open arms, I welcome more,
May abundance reach my door."

◈ **Result:** Within weeks, you will notice **new doors opening in your life**.

Conclusion: Living in the Flow of Gratitude and Abundance

The **Principle of Gratitude and Abundance** reminds us that we are **already rich in ways we may not see**. When we **honor what we have**, we ensure **more is always on the way**.

By **partnering with the spirits of ancient Earth, shifting our mindset, and practicing sacred gratitude**, we align with the **eternal flow of prosperity**.

The dinosaurs knew abundance in their time—and so shall we, in ours. ◈◈

Chapter 10: The Principle of Protection and Boundaries

Protection is one of the most fundamental aspects of any spiritual path. Just as dinosaurs developed **armor, defensive structures, and powerful survival instincts**, so too must we learn how to protect ourselves—both physically and spiritually. In **Dino Wicca**, the **Principle of Protection and Boundaries** teaches us how to **shield our energy, set strong personal limits, and invoke prehistoric guardians for safety.**

The world of the dinosaurs was **full of challenges**—predators lurking, shifting landscapes, and constant environmental changes. Yet, many species **adapted powerful defenses** to survive. Some, like the **Stegosaurus**, developed armored plates; others, like the **Triceratops**, had mighty horns to ward off threats; and still others, like the **Ankylosaurus**, wielded clubbed tails as weapons of protection. **We, too, can call upon these ancient energies to create spiritual armor and establish firm boundaries.**

By learning how to **shield ourselves from negative energy, set firm emotional and spiritual boundaries, and perform powerful protection spells**, we ensure that we walk the Dino Wiccan path **with strength, safety, and sovereignty.**

Shielding Yourself with Dino Wiccan Magick

Every being, from the smallest insect to the mightiest dinosaur, has some form of **protective instinct**. In the **modern world, our threats may not be physical predators, but rather energy vampires, emotional manipulation, negativity, and spiritual attacks.** This is where **Dino Wiccan shielding magick** becomes essential.

1. Creating an Energetic Dino Shield

To shield yourself, you must first visualize an **energetic barrier** surrounding you. This shield can be inspired by **prehistoric creatures** known for their **defense mechanisms**.

The Stegosaurus Shield (Full-Body Protection)

The **Stegosaurus** was covered in **bony plates**, forming a natural armor. We can invoke this energy to create **a powerful, impenetrable shield** around ourselves.

◈ **How to Create the Stegosaurus Shield:**

1. Stand or sit comfortably and **close your eyes**.
2. Imagine **plates of energy forming along your back and sides**, just like a Stegosaurus.
3. Say aloud:

"With armor strong and shields raised high,
No harm shall pass, no fear am I.
Stegosaurus, wise and true,
Guard my path in all I do."

1. Feel the **plates absorbing and deflecting negativity**.

Use this shield when:

- You are in **crowded places** where energy may overwhelm you.
- You feel **emotionally vulnerable** or need **spiritual protection**.

The Triceratops Boundary (Defending Personal Space)
The **Triceratops** used its **three sharp horns** to **defend itself and establish territory**. In Dino Wicca, we can **channel this energy to set firm personal boundaries.**
⟡ **How to Set a Triceratops Boundary:**

1. Hold a **stone or crystal** that represents strength (**black tourmaline, obsidian, or tiger's eye**).
2. Close your eyes and **visualize three great horns of light extending outward from your energy field**.
3. Say aloud:

"With horns of strength, I claim my space,
No ill shall cross, no harm I face.
Boundaries firm, my will is set,
In Triceratops' strength, no threat is met."

1. Open your eyes and **carry the charged crystal with you** as a **symbol of your personal boundaries**.

Use this technique when:

- You need to **say no** to emotional, mental, or energetic drains.
- You feel someone is **pushing past your limits**.
- You need **to stand strong against manipulation or intimidation**.

Setting Healthy Emotional and Spiritual Boundaries

Boundaries are not just about **keeping danger away**—they are about **honoring our own limits, knowing our worth, and protecting our energy. Even the mightiest dinosaurs had territories and limits**—so should we.

Signs You Need Stronger Boundaries

- You feel **exhausted after being around certain people.**
- You struggle to **say no without guilt.**
- You feel **pressured to do things you don't want to.**
- People **take advantage of your kindness.**
- You feel **mentally and emotionally drained** after conversations.

How to Strengthen Boundaries the Dino Wiccan Way:

- **Identify what drains your energy.** If something **makes you feel uneasy, exhausted, or overwhelmed**, it may require stronger boundaries.
- **Use protective symbols**—wearing fossils, carrying talismans, or using natural elements **can strengthen your energy field.**
- **Be firm in your decisions.** Just like a **Tyrannosaurus wouldn't hesitate to claim its space, neither should you.**
- **Limit access to your energy.** Not everyone **deserves your time, love, and attention**—choose wisely who gets access to your sacred space.

Spells for Protection and Safety

Now that we understand **shielding and boundaries**, let's explore **three powerful Dino Wiccan spells** for protection.

1. The Ankylosaurus Armor Spell (Total Protection) ◈

The **Ankylosaurus** was a **walking fortress**, with **thick armor and a powerful clubbed tail**. This spell **fortifies your energy**, creating an **impenetrable field** around you.

Materials:

- A **black candle** (for protection)
- A **small stone or fossil** (to charge with protective energy)
- A bowl of **salt**

◈ **How to Perform the Spell:**

1. **Light the black candle**, focusing on **drawing strength from the Earth**.
2. **Hold the stone or fossil** and visualize it **becoming infused with the protective power of the Ankylosaurus.**
3. Say:

"Like the armored beast of old,
My shield is strong, my ground is bold.
No harm may touch, no fear may stay,
I walk in strength, night and day."

1. Place the **stone in the bowl of salt overnight** to solidify its power.
2. Carry the **charged stone** with you for ongoing protection.

◈ **Result:** You will feel **more grounded, resilient, and shielded from negativity**.

2. The Pterosaur Flight Spell (Escape from Toxic Situations) ◈

The **Pterosaurs** were the **masters of flight**, using their wings to **soar above danger**. This spell helps you **remove yourself from unhealthy situations with ease**.

Materials:

- A **white feather or light stone**
- A **blue candle** (symbolizing air and freedom)

◈ **How to Perform the Spell:**

1. Light the **blue candle** and hold the **feather or stone** in your hands.
2. Close your eyes and **visualize yourself soaring above obstacles**, just like a Pterosaur.
3. Say:

"Wings of sky, swift and free,
Lift me high, away from thee.
Where harm may lie, I will not stay,
I rise above, I fly away."

1. Blow out the candle and **release the feather or bury the stone**, symbolizing your escape from toxic energy.

◈ **Result:** You will find yourself **naturally distancing from toxic people and situations with ease.**

3. The T. Rex Guardian Spell (Protection Against Psychic Attacks) ◈

The **Tyrannosaurus Rex** was an apex predator—**no one messed with it**. This spell **calls upon its energy to shield you from spiritual or psychic attacks**.

Materials:

- A **red candle**
- A piece of **iron, obsidian, or tiger's eye**
- A **mirror**

◈ **How to Perform the Spell:**

1. **Light the red candle** and place the mirror in front of you.
2. Hold the **stone** in your dominant hand and say:

"Mighty king, strong and bold,
Your fire shields, your power holds.
No curse nor ill shall pass to me,
My spirit strong, my soul set free!"

1. Blow out the candle and **carry the stone for ongoing protection**.

◈ **Result:** You will feel **more secure, grounded, and immune to negativity**.

Conclusion: Walking Strong, Guarded, and Free

The **Principle of Protection and Boundaries** ensures that we **walk the path of Dino Wicca in strength, wisdom, and safety**. By using **shielding techniques, setting clear boundaries, and working with powerful protection spells**, we **fortify our energy** and **walk boldly through life, just as the great dinosaurs once did.** ◈◈

Chapter 11: The Principle of Cyclical Renewal

Life is a cycle of **beginnings, transformations, and endings**—but nothing truly ends. **The old gives way to the new, just as the dinosaurs evolved, lived, and left behind echoes of their existence in the form of fossils, their energy forever imprinted on the Earth.** In **Dino Wicca**, the **Principle of Cyclical Renewal** teaches us to **embrace life's natural cycles**—from birth to death, from growth to decay, and from old ways of being into new forms of transformation.

Dinosaurs lived through massive evolutionary shifts, adapting to **Earth's ever-changing environments**, surviving for over **165 million years** before their extinction. But their legacy did not vanish—their DNA continued in birds, their fossils remained to teach us about the past, and their presence still exists in **the great cycle of the Earth's history. Likewise, we are never truly at an ending—only moving into a new form of existence.**

By honoring the **seasons, the cycles of life and death, and the constant transformation within ourselves**, we step into the **eternal rhythm of nature. Cyclical renewal is not just about survival—it is about evolution, embracing change, and using nature's wisdom to guide our own personal rebirths.**

Embracing Life's Cycles of Death and Rebirth

The natural world is constantly shifting—**life emerges, grows, declines, and renews itself once more.** Dinosaurs thrived for millions of years, yet they eventually faded, making way for **new life, new species, and new ecosystems.** This teaches us that **change is not an enemy, but a natural process of existence.**

1. The Dinosaur Extinction and the Meaning of Rebirth

The great extinction event that ended the reign of the dinosaurs was **not the end of life**—it was the beginning of a **new world, new creatures, and new possibilities.** In our own lives, we face **smaller extinctions**—the loss of relationships, careers, old versions of ourselves—but these are always followed by **rebirth into something greater.**

◈ **Key Lesson:** Instead of fearing endings, **see them as a gateway to transformation.** Just as the Earth did not end when the dinosaurs vanished, **we, too, continue forward into new cycles of growth.**

2. Personal Cycles of Change

We experience **cycles of death and rebirth** in many ways:

- The **death of old habits,** making way for **new, healthier ways of living.**
- The **end of toxic relationships,** allowing space for **new, nourishing connections.**
- The **conclusion of a phase in life,** leading to **a new adventure or opportunity.**

Just as the Earth **recycles its energy,** we must learn to **let go of what no longer serves us, trusting that something better is always forming.**

Dino Wiccan Celebrations of Seasonal Changes

Just as dinosaurs **adapted to environmental shifts**, we, too, must learn to **honor the cycles of nature** by observing **seasonal changes and the renewal of life**.

1. The Four Major Dino Wiccan Seasonal Festivals

Each season marks a **shift in energy, a new phase of growth, and a chance to realign with the Earth.**

Season	Dino Wiccan Meaning	Key Celebration Ritual
Spring Equinox (The Hatchling's Dawn)	New beginnings, rebirth, fresh energy	Planting seeds, setting new intentions
Summer Solstice (The Apex Roar)	Strength, full energy, peak potential	Fire ceremonies, personal empowerment rituals
Autumn Equinox (The Great Migration)	Harvest, reflection, transition	Giving thanks, preparing for inward spiritual work
Winter Solstice (The Fossil's Rest)	Stillness, introspection, transformation	Shadow work, honoring the past and planning the future

The Hatchling's Dawn (Spring Equinox) ◈

- Symbolizes **new life**, like **a dinosaur egg hatching** after incubation.
- A time to **set goals, make fresh starts, and welcome renewal.**

◈ Ritual: Egg of Transformation

1. Write down **a new goal** on a small piece of paper.
2. Place it inside an **egg-shaped stone or in a nest of leaves**.
3. Speak:

"As the hatchling breaks the shell,
So shall my path unfold as well."

1. Leave the egg on your altar until your goal starts manifesting.

The Apex Roar (Summer Solstice) ⟡

- Celebrates **peak energy and personal power**, like **a mighty dinosaur standing at its strongest.**
- A time to **embrace courage, confidence, and strength** in all aspects of life.

⟡ Ritual: Roar of Strength Ceremony

1. Light a **gold or red candle** to symbolize the **power of the sun.**
2. Stand with feet firmly planted, taking a **deep breath.**
3. Visualize yourself as **a strong dinosaur**, roaring in triumph.
4. Say:

"At my peak, I stand tall,
I claim my strength, I will not fall."

1. Let the candle burn safely as you **absorb the energy of power and resilience.**

The Great Migration (Autumn Equinox) ⟡

- Just as some dinosaurs **migrated during seasonal changes**, we prepare for **inner transformation and reflection.**
- A time to **harvest lessons learned and express gratitude**.

⟡ Ritual: The Fossilized Wisdom Ceremony

1. Collect **three small stones** (symbolizing ancient wisdom).
2. Hold each one and think about a lesson **you've learned this year.**
3. Say:

"Like fossils deep beneath the sand,
I hold this wisdom in my hand."

1. Keep the stones on your altar **as reminders of your growth.**

The Fossil's Rest (Winter Solstice) ◈

- Represents **the quiet of the Earth,** like **dinosaur fossils lying in deep slumber beneath the soil.**
- A time for **introspection, shadow work, and preparing for the next cycle.**

◈ Ritual: Burial of the Old Year

1. Write down what you **wish to release** on a piece of biodegradable paper.
2. Bury it in the ground, saying:

"Rest now, fade away,
Make space for a brighter day."

1. Give thanks for the lessons learned and **prepare for new growth.**

Using the Cycles of Nature for Personal Renewal
1. Letting Go of What No Longer Serves You

- Just as **dinosaurs shed old behaviors** to evolve, we must **release what holds us back.**
- Write a **list of things you are ready to release** and burn it in a safe fire to **symbolize transformation.**

2. Trusting the Process of Change

- Change can be **frightening, but necessary.**
- Remember that **the dinosaurs did not resist the flow of time**—they adapted.
- Meditate on **the resilience of prehistoric creatures** and remind yourself that **you, too, can survive any transition.**

3. Setting Intentions for Renewal

- Align your **goals with the seasons**—start new projects in spring, build in summer, reflect in autumn, and rest in winter.
- Use fossils as **symbols of wisdom,** reminding you that **growth takes time but is always happening.**

Conclusion: Living in Harmony with Cyclical Renewal

The **Principle of Cyclical Renewal** reminds us that life is **not a straight path—it is a spiral, constantly evolving, shifting, and transforming.** By honoring **the cycles of nature, embracing change, and using rituals to realign with prehistoric wisdom**, we step into a **life of balance, wisdom, and renewal.**

Like the dinosaurs before us, we will evolve, grow, and leave behind a legacy of strength and resilience. ◇◇

Chapter 12: The Principle of Love and Unity

Love is one of the most **primal, ancient, and sacred forces in existence**. It is the energy that binds the universe together, the force that fuels growth, and the **foundation of community, connection, and harmony**. In **Dino Wicca**, the **Principle of Love and Unity** teaches that **love is more than just an emotion—it is a universal law, a sacred bond that connects all beings, from the prehistoric past to the present moment.**

Dinosaurs, much like modern animals, formed **social groups, cared for their young, and worked together for survival**. Fossil evidence suggests that some species, like the **Maiasaura**, nurtured their offspring with great care, while others, such as **Pachycephalosaurus**, engaged in bonding behaviors. This tells us that **love, connection, and unity were not foreign concepts in the ancient world**—they were vital aspects of existence.

As Dino Wiccans, we honor love as a **sacred force that unites all living beings**. We learn to cultivate love in all its forms—**self-love, romantic love, friendship, community, and universal love**—while also strengthening the bonds that connect us to the **Earth, the spirits of prehistoric wisdom, and the cycles of life.**

This chapter will explore:

◈ **Honoring love as a powerful force in Dino Wicca**
◈ **Building strong relationships and spiritual bonds**
◈ **Rituals to deepen connections with others and yourself**

Honoring Love as a Powerful Force in Dino Wicca

In Dino Wicca, love is seen as **one of the strongest magickal energies in the universe**. It is a **binding force** that:

- Connects us to nature, the Earth, and ancient energies.
- Forms the foundation of relationships, families, and friendships.
- Strengthens our ability to heal, grow, and evolve.
- Encourages unity between individuals, communities, and all living beings.

1. The Different Forms of Love in Dino Wicca

Love comes in many forms, and each plays a unique role in our spiritual journey:

Type of Love	Dino Wiccan Meaning	How to Cultivate It
Self-Love	Honoring oneself, accepting personal strengths and flaws.	Daily affirmations, self-care rituals, self-forgiveness.
Romantic Love	A bond between partners based on trust, passion, and respect.	Strengthening emotional connections, shared rituals.
Friendship & Community Love	Love between friends, family, and kindred spirits.	Acts of kindness, gratitude, community gatherings.
Universal Love	Love for the Earth, ancestors, and all life.	Offering gratitude to nature, working in harmony with the planet.

Building Strong Relationships and Spiritual Bonds

Love does not exist in isolation—it grows through **connection, communication, and mutual care**. Just as prehistoric creatures **formed herds, packs, and families** for survival, we too thrive when we **nurture strong relationships** with ourselves and those around us.

1. Strengthening Your Relationship with Yourself

Before we can build strong bonds with others, we must first **cultivate a deep love for ourselves**. Self-love is **not arrogance or selfishness**—it is the foundation of self-worth, confidence, and inner peace.

⬥ **Dino Wiccan Self-Love Practices:**

- **The Fossil Reflection Ritual:** Hold a fossil in your hands and meditate on the idea that **you, too, are an ancient soul with a long history of growth and transformation.**
- **Daily Affirmations:** Speak words of love to yourself, such as:

"I honor my strength, my wisdom, my path."

- **Cleansing Rituals:** Bathe in **saltwater or herbal infusions** to release negativity and **embrace self-renewal**.

2. Strengthening Romantic and Emotional Bonds

Love between partners is **a sacred bond, one that thrives when nurtured with respect, passion, and shared energy**.

⬥ **Dino Wiccan Practices for Romantic Love:**

- **Moonlit Connection Ritual:** Spend time **under the moon** with your partner, holding hands and sharing your dreams for the future.
- **Elemental Bonding:** Work with the **four elements** to strengthen your relationship:
    - **Earth** – Build a strong foundation of trust.
    - **Water** – Encourage emotional depth and understanding.
    - **Fire** – Ignite passion and adventure.
    - **Air** – Improve communication and mental connection.
- **Create Shared Sacred Space:** Design an **altar together**, placing items that symbolize your love—a fossil, a candle, a handwritten note.

3. Strengthening Friendships and Community Bonds

Love is **not just romantic—it extends to our friendships, families, and spiritual communities**. Dino Wiccans honor love by **building strong, meaningful connections** with others.

◈ **Dino Wiccan Community Rituals:**

- **Gathering Circles:** Host **seasonal celebrations**, inviting friends and loved ones to share a meal and gratitude.
- **The Fossil Exchange:** Gift a **small fossil or stone** to a friend as a symbol of **enduring connection and shared wisdom**.
- **Protection Rituals:** Perform a **group protection spell** to safeguard **each other's energy and wellbeing**.

By **nurturing bonds with friends and the spiritual community**, we **recreate the unity of prehistoric herds and clans**, ensuring that **no one walks alone.**

Rituals to Deepen Connections with Others and Yourself

1. The Heartbeat of the Earth Ritual (Universal Love Ceremony)

Purpose: To connect with **the universal love that flows through the Earth, the ancestors, and all life**.

Materials:

- A **stone or fossil** (symbolizing the ancient heart of the world)
- A **green or pink candle**
- A **bowl of water**

◈ **Steps:**

1. **Sit in a quiet place** and hold the **fossil or stone** close to your heart.
2. Light the **green or pink candle**, saying:

"Ancient heart, beating strong,
Love unites us, all along.
From past to now, from land to sky,
May love's great power never die."

1. Place the **stone in the bowl of water**, symbolizing the **flow of love through time**.
2. Meditate on **sending love outward**—to yourself, your family, your ancestors, and the world.
3. Leave the stone in the water overnight as a **symbol of love's eternal presence**.

2. The Dino Love Bonding Spell (Strengthening Romantic & Friendship Bonds)

Purpose: To strengthen a bond with a loved one, **deepening trust, love, and unity**.

Materials:

- Two **fossils or stones** (one for you, one for your loved one)
- A **red, pink, or gold candle**
- A **small piece of string or ribbon**

◈ **Steps:**

1. Sit across from your **partner, friend, or family member**, each holding a **fossil or stone**.
2. Light the **candle** and say together:

"Bound by time, strong as stone,
Our bond shall stand, love is known."

1. **Tie the two fossils together with the ribbon**, sealing the bond.

2. Each person keeps **one stone**, a reminder of the **sacred connection.**

Conclusion: Walking the Path of Love and Unity

The **Principle of Love and Unity** teaches that love is **not just an emotion—it is the sacred force that binds all things**. Whether it is **self-love, romantic love, friendship, or universal love**, we honor this energy by **nurturing connections, practicing gratitude, and strengthening our bonds with others.**

By walking this path, we **echo the great herds of the past**, ensuring that **no one walks alone, and love remains the guiding force of our existence.** ◈ ◈ ◈

Chapter 13: The Principle of Legacy and Remembrance

The world we live in is shaped by those who came before us. From the towering dinosaurs that once ruled the Earth to the ancestors whose knowledge flows through our bloodline, **every being leaves behind a legacy**—a mark on the land, in history, and in the energy of the universe.

In **Dino Wicca**, the **Principle of Legacy and Remembrance** teaches that we are **not just individuals moving through time**; we are **part of a vast lineage, stretching from the ancient past into the distant future. Just as fossils preserve the stories of prehistoric creatures, our actions, wisdom, and magickal work will live on long after we are gone.**

By honoring **the spirits of the past, preserving ancestral knowledge, and consciously shaping the spiritual world for future generations**, we ensure that the wisdom of Dino Wicca is never lost. This chapter will explore:

◈ **How to leave a spiritual imprint for future generations.**
◈ **Ways to honor ancestors and Dino spirits.**
◈ **Practices for passing down Dino Wiccan wisdom.**

Leaving a Spiritual Imprint for Future Generations

Every species leaves a trace of its existence. Some leave **fossils buried in the Earth**, while others leave **genetic legacies, traditions, or spiritual wisdom**. In Dino Wicca, we believe that **our energy, actions, and magickal practices carry forward into the future**, influencing those who come after us.

1. Understanding Your Spiritual Legacy

Legacy is not just about **physical objects**—it is about the **impact we make on the spiritual and energetic world**.

Ask yourself:

- What knowledge, wisdom, or energy do I wish to pass down?
- How can I ensure that the teachings of **Dino Wicca** live on?
- What imprint am I leaving on the world, both in my personal life and spiritual practice?

Just as dinosaurs **left behind fossils, tracks, and remnants of their existence**, we, too, leave behind **energetic and spiritual markers. Our practices, teachings, and rituals will serve as guiding lights for future seekers.**

Honoring Ancestors and Dino Spirits

Legacy does not begin with us—it is part of a **chain of existence**, stretching back through time. **By honoring those who came before us, we deepen our understanding of our place in the world and strengthen the spiritual path of Dino Wicca.**

1. The Ancestors of Blood and Spirit

In Dino Wicca, ancestors are not only those **related to us by blood** but also those **connected through shared wisdom and energy.** This includes:

- **Family ancestors** (relatives who have passed on).
- **Spiritual ancestors** (mentors, teachers, and past practitioners of Earth-based traditions).
- **Ancient Earth ancestors** (prehistoric beings, dinosaurs, and early life forms that shaped the world).

By recognizing that **we are part of an unbroken line of existence**, we create **a living connection between past, present, and future.**

2. Ritual to Honor Ancestors and Prehistoric Spirits

Purpose: To honor the wisdom of the past and seek guidance from ancestors and Dino spirits.
Materials:

- A **fossil, stone, or earth from an ancient place**
- A **white or black candle**
- A **bowl of water** (symbolizing the flow of time)
- An **offering** (such as seeds, herbs, or symbolic items)

◈ **Steps:**

1. **Light the candle** and place the fossil or stone in front of you.
2. Gaze into the **bowl of water**, imagining it as a portal to the past.
3. Say:

"Spirits of time, old and wise,
Guide my steps with ancient ties.
Ancestors strong, and beasts of old,
Your wisdom flows, your stories told."

1. Hold the fossil in your hands, **feeling the energy of the past flowing into you.**
2. Make an **offering** to the spirits, placing the seeds or herbs on the Earth.
3. Close the ritual by thanking the spirits:

"Through time we walk, from past to now,
With wisdom bright, this I vow."

◈ **Result:** You will feel a **deepened connection to ancestral energies** and an **increased awareness of your place in the cosmic lineage.**

Practices for Passing Down Dino Wiccan Wisdom

One of the most important aspects of **legacy and remembrance** is **ensuring that the wisdom of Dino Wicca continues** for future generations. Just as **dinosaurs passed their instincts to their offspring**, we, too, pass **knowledge, rituals, and magickal practices** to those who come after us.

1. The Written Legacy: Creating a Dino Wiccan Grimoire

A **grimoire** or **Book of Shadows** is a **sacred text** where we record our rituals, experiences, and knowledge. To ensure that **Dino Wiccan traditions live on**, consider:

- **Writing down your spells, meditations, and rituals.**
- **Including personal experiences with Dino spirits.**
- **Documenting seasonal celebrations and personal discoveries.**
- **Creating a family or community tradition that can be passed down.**

◇ Fossil Magick Tip: Press a **fossil imprint** onto your book's cover or pages to **infuse it with the energy of ancient wisdom.**

2. Oral Tradition: Sharing Dino Wiccan Stories and Teachings

Before written records, **wisdom was passed down through storytelling.** Consider:

- **Telling stories of your spiritual journey** to friends, students, or loved ones.
- **Creating rituals where knowledge is shared in spoken form.**
- **Teaching others about the cycles of nature, prehistoric wisdom, and Earth-based spirituality.**

By keeping the **oral tradition alive,** you ensure that **Dino Wicca is not just written, but lived.**

3. Ritual of Spiritual Inheritance: Passing Down Dino Wiccan Wisdom

Purpose: To pass knowledge, wisdom, and spiritual energy to another seeker or future generation.

Materials:

- A **fossil, crystal, or sacred object**
- A **candle of any color that represents wisdom**
- A **written blessing or lesson**

◈ **Steps:**

1. Light the candle and hold the **fossil or sacred object** in your hands.
2. Reflect on **the wisdom you wish to pass down**—this may be to a specific person or to the **universal energy of the future.**
3. Say:

"From past to now, from now to then,
Wisdom flows and grows again.
As fossils hold the tales of time,
May this knowledge forever shine."

1. Place the **written blessing inside a book, box, or envelope** and store it in a safe place.
2. Pass the **fossil or object to its new guardian** or **bury it in the Earth to serve as a spiritual time capsule.**

◈ **Result:** This act **creates a magickal bond between generations**, ensuring that the **Dino Wiccan path continues beyond your lifetime.**

Conclusion: Walking in the Footsteps of the Ancient Ones

The **Principle of Legacy and Remembrance** teaches that we are **part of something far greater than ourselves.** Just as the dinosaurs left their **marks on the world through fossils, tracks, and evolutionary lines**, we, too, leave **our spiritual imprints in the world of magick and wisdom.**

By honoring our ancestors, recording our knowledge, and **passing down the sacred path of Dino Wicca**, we ensure that our teachings will **never fade—but instead will continue to guide future generations, just as the great beasts of old once roamed the Earth.** ◈◈

Appendix A: Dino Wicca Glossary

This glossary serves as a **comprehensive guide to key terms and concepts in Dino Wicca**. Whether you are new to the path or a seasoned practitioner, these definitions will help deepen your understanding of the **sacred connection between prehistoric wisdom, magick, and modern spiritual practice**.

A

Ancestral Spirits

The spirits of those who came before us, including both **human ancestors and the ancient prehistoric beings** that shaped the Earth's evolution. Dino Wiccans often honor these spirits in rituals to gain wisdom and guidance.

Ancient Cycles

The **ever-repeating patterns of time, nature, and energy**—such as **the migration of dinosaurs, the shifting of the Earth's landmasses, and the rhythms of the sun and moon**—that influence all aspects of Dino Wiccan practice.

Animism

The belief that **all things, including animals, plants, fossils, and even landscapes, possess a spirit or consciousness**. This concept is central to Dino Wicca, as it teaches that dinosaurs and ancient Earth energies are still present in the spiritual realm.

B

Bone Magick

The practice of using **fossils, bones, or representations of prehistoric creatures** to connect with ancient wisdom, protection, and spiritual grounding. This can include **carrying a fossil for strength, using it in rituals, or meditating with it to access ancestral knowledge**.

Boundaries (Spiritual and Emotional)

The energetic and emotional **barriers we set to protect ourselves from harm, negativity, or unwanted influences**. In Dino Wicca, boundaries are reinforced through **shielding techniques, protective spells, and channeling the resilience of armored dinosaurs like Ankylosaurus or Triceratops**.

C

Celestial Alignments

The **positioning of celestial bodies** (such as the moon, sun, and planets) that influence energy patterns and magickal workings. Dino Wiccans align their **rituals with these cosmic forces**, just as prehistoric creatures once followed celestial rhythms for migration, reproduction, and survival.

Co-Creation (Magickal)

The concept of working **in partnership with spiritual forces, dinosaur spirits, and Earth's energy** to manifest intentions. Dino Wiccans believe that by collaborating with these forces, their magickal workings are strengthened and aligned with the **natural cycles of the universe**.

Cyclical Renewal

The principle that **all things exist in cycles—birth, growth, death, and rebirth**. Just as dinosaurs evolved and new species emerged, **personal and spiritual transformation follows this sacred rhythm**. Dino Wiccans use this concept in rituals for **new beginnings, healing, and releasing the past**.

D

Dino Spirits

The **energetic remnants of prehistoric creatures** that can serve as guides, protectors, and teachers in the Dino Wiccan path. Each species carries a **unique magickal energy**—for example, T. rex represents **strength and leadership**, while Pteranodon embodies **freedom and higher knowledge**.

Dino Totem

A **dinosaur spirit or species** that serves as a personal guide and source of wisdom. Dino Wiccans often meditate or perform rituals to discover which **dino totem** aligns with their personal energy and life path.

Dinomancy

A form of **divination using dinosaur-related objects**, such as **fossils, tracks, bones, or prehistoric symbols**, to receive messages from the past or guidance for the future.

E

Earth Magick

A practice that focuses on using the **elements of the natural world (soil, fossils, stones, water, and plants) to enhance spiritual energy**. Dino Wicca places great emphasis on **working with ancient Earth energies** to honor the prehistoric past.

Extinction as Transformation

The belief that **extinction is not the end, but rather a transition into a new phase of existence**. Just as dinosaurs **evolved into modern birds**, personal transformation is viewed as an **ongoing journey of adaptation and growth**.

F

Fossil Magick

The use of **fossils in spiritual practice** to connect with **prehistoric energy, ancient wisdom, and the endurance of time**. Fossils can be used for **protection, meditation, or as talismans for grounding and strength**.

Fossil Offering

A ritual practice in which **a fossil, stone, or symbolic object is offered to the Earth** as a sign of **gratitude and connection to ancient spirits**.

G

Grounding

A technique used to **stabilize one's energy by connecting with the Earth**, much like how dinosaurs were deeply rooted in their environments. Grounding can be done through **walking barefoot, holding fossils, or meditating with ancient stones**.

H

Herbology (Prehistoric Plant Magick)

The use of **herbs, plants, and tree resins that existed during the age of the dinosaurs** in magickal workings. Dino Wiccans often incorporate **ferns, cycads, and pine resin** into rituals for **healing, protection, and connection to ancient energies**.

Herd Energy

The concept of **working within a supportive group or community**, inspired by the way many dinosaurs thrived in **herds or packs**. This energy is used in **group rituals, community healing, and building strong spiritual connections**.

L

Ley Lines (Earth's Energy Paths)

Natural **energetic pathways** that crisscross the Earth, believed to be **connected to ancient power centers**. Dino Wiccans recognize these **ley lines as part of the planet's memory, linking prehistoric times to modern spiritual practices**.

Legacy Magick

The practice of **preserving and passing down Dino Wiccan knowledge, rituals, and spiritual teachings** for future generations. This is often done through **creating a Book of Dino Shadows, storytelling, or writing letters to future seekers**.

M

Meteorite Magick

The use of **meteorites and celestial stones** in rituals to connect with the **cosmic forces that shaped the prehistoric world**. Dino Wiccans believe that **meteorites hold ancient wisdom from the stars**.

P

Prehistoric Wisdom

The knowledge and **energetic imprints** left behind by **ancient Earth, dinosaurs, and evolutionary cycles**, which can be accessed through meditation, dreams, and spiritual work.

Protection Rituals

Magickal workings designed to **shield oneself from negative energies**, often inspired by the **defensive adaptations of dinosaurs like Triceratops (boundaries), Ankylosaurus (armor), and Stegosaurus (energetic shielding).**

S

Sacred Fossils

Fossils that have been **consecrated or blessed** for use in spiritual practice. These may be used in **rituals, altars, or as protective talismans**.

Seasonal Dino Celebrations

Dino Wiccan festivals that align with the **changing of the seasons**, honoring the prehistoric world's connection to **Earth's cycles** (e.g., **The Hatchling's Dawn (Spring), The Apex Roar (Summer), The Great Migration (Autumn), and The Fossil's Rest (Winter)**).

T

Tyrannosaurus Energy

The energy of **confidence, power, and leadership**, inspired by the T. rex. Used in rituals for **self-empowerment, overcoming fear, and asserting personal strength**.

V

Velociraptor Strategy

A concept used in **Dino Wiccan decision-making**, emphasizing **intelligence, quick thinking, and adaptability**, much like the **Velociraptor's hunting tactics**.

W

Wheel of Prehistoric Time

The **cyclical understanding of time** in Dino Wicca, reflecting **evolution, adaptation, and spiritual transformation** rather than linear time.

Conclusion

This **Dino Wicca Glossary** serves as a **foundational guide** for understanding the key terms, concepts, and magickal philosophies of the path. As you walk this **prehistoric-inspired spiritual journey**, let these words **deepen your practice, guide your rituals, and connect you with the ancient past.** ◇◇

Appendix B: Sacred Dino Wicca Rituals

This appendix provides **step-by-step rituals** to practice the **13 Sacred Principles of Dino Wicca**. Each ritual aligns with one of the principles, allowing practitioners to **deepen their connection to prehistoric wisdom, ancient Earth energies, and spiritual growth.** These rituals can be performed **individually or in groups**, using fossils, natural elements, and sacred intent to honor the legacy of the dinosaurs and the cycles of time.

1. The Ritual of Universal Acceptance

◈ **For: Embracing diversity and unity within Dino Wicca.**

Materials:

- A **multicolored stone** (symbolizing different energies coming together)
- A **white candle** (unity and acceptance)
- A bowl of **salt water** (purification)

◈ **Steps:**

1. Light the **white candle**, focusing on the flame as a **symbol of universal acceptance**.
2. Hold the **multicolored stone** and say:

"From the past to now, we stand as one,
No soul denied, no heart undone.
In love, I welcome, in peace, I see,
The sacred bond of unity."

1. Dip your fingers in the **salt water**, touching your forehead, heart, and palms, saying:

"I cleanse judgment, I embrace the whole."

1. Place the stone on your altar as a **reminder of inclusivity**.

2. The Ritual of Respect for All Living Things
◈ **For: Honoring life in all its forms, from insects to great dinosaurs.**
Materials:

- A **small plant or tree sapling**
- A bowl of **fresh water**
- A **symbol of prehistoric life** (fossil, stone, or feather)

◈ **Steps:**

1. Hold the **symbol of prehistoric life**, honoring the creatures that once roamed the Earth.
2. Say:

"From the smallest to the grand,
Life is sacred, hand in hand.
I honor all, in Earth's embrace,
Respecting each in time and space."

1. Pour the **fresh water onto the plant**, symbolizing **nourishment for life**.
2. Place the **symbol of prehistoric life** on your altar, reaffirming your respect for all creatures.

3. The Ritual of Connection to Prehistoric Wisdom
◈ **For:** Tapping into ancient energies and learning from Dino spirits.

Materials:

- A **fossil or ancient stone**
- A **blue candle** (representing knowledge)
- A bowl of **earth or sand**

◈ **Steps:**

1. Hold the **fossil** in your hands, closing your eyes and visualizing **dinosaurs walking across an ancient land**.
2. Light the **blue candle**, saying:

"Ancient ones, old and wise,
Lend your sight, your truth, your ties.
From fossils deep and wisdom bright,
Reveal your lessons, share your light."

1. Meditate for a few minutes, **listening for messages** or insights.
2. Write down your experience in a **sacred journal** to reflect on later.

4. The Ritual of Evolution and Personal Growth
◈ For: Embracing change and growth in life.
Materials:

- A **cocoon-like object** (shell, egg, or stone)
- A **mirror**
- A **green candle** (symbolizing transformation)

◈ **Steps:**

1. Light the **green candle**, gazing into the flame as a symbol of **evolution**.
2. Hold the **cocoon-like object**, saying:

"Like the beasts of time before,
I evolve, I change, I grow once more.
No fear shall bind, no doubt shall stay,
I rise anew, I find my way."

1. Look into the **mirror** and **affirm your willingness to embrace change**.
2. Keep the **object on your altar** as a **symbol of growth**.

5. The Ritual of Harmony with the Earth
⟡ **For: Strengthening your connection to nature.**
Materials:

- A **handful of soil or natural earth**
- A **small bowl of water**
- A **leaf, stone, or fossil**

⟡ **Steps:**

1. Stand barefoot on the ground, holding the **soil in one hand** and the **water in the other**.
2. Say:

"Earth and water, old and wise,
Keep me grounded, harmonized.
As dinosaurs roamed, free and wild,
May I walk as nature's child."

1. Pour the **water onto the soil**, mixing them together to symbolize **unity with nature**.
2. Scatter the soil back onto the Earth, giving **thanks for the land that sustains all life**.

6. The Ritual of Courage and Strength
◈ **For: Overcoming fear and building inner resilience.**
Materials:

- A **T. rex figurine or fossil** (symbolizing strength)
- A **red candle**
- A **piece of iron or stone**

◈ **Steps:**

1. Light the **red candle**, focusing on the flame as a **symbol of bravery**.
2. Hold the **T. rex symbol** and say:

"With mighty roar and fearless stride,
I stand in strength, I cast fear aside.
As the T. rex ruled the land,
I take my place, I take my stand."

1. Hold the **iron or stone**, absorbing **its solid energy**.
2. Carry the object with you as a **reminder of your courage**.

7. The Ritual of Sacred Time and Space
◈ **For: Creating a sacred Dino Wiccan altar.**
Materials:

- A **small dinosaur figure, fossil, or stone**
- A **candle of any color**
- A bowl of **salt (for purification)**

◈ **Steps:**

1. Cleanse your altar space with **salt**, removing negative energy.
2. Place the **dinosaur figure/fossil** at the center, saying:

"Sacred space, now set apart,
In time and spirit, in soul and heart.
From past to now, from now to then,
This space is holy once again."

1. Light the **candle**, welcoming **sacred energy** into your space.

8. The Ritual of Magickal Co-Creation
◈ **For: Manifesting desires with Dino spirit guidance.**
Materials:

- A **fossil** (connection to ancient energy)
- A **gold or green candle** (prosperity & manifestation)
- A written **goal or desire**

◈ **Steps:**

1. Light the **candle** and hold the **fossil**, focusing on your goal.
2. Say:

"With Earth's wisdom and spirits old,
My vision shapes, my will takes hold.
With Dino strength, I set this free,
So mote it be!"

1. Burn or bury the **written goal**, symbolizing its **release into the universe**.

9. The Ritual of Gratitude and Abundance
◈ **For: Cultivating thankfulness and attracting prosperity.**
Materials:

- A **bowl of seeds or grains** (symbolizing abundance)
- A **yellow or gold candle**
- A **small fossil or stone** (representing Earth's gifts)

◈ **Steps:**

1. Light the **yellow/gold candle**, focusing on the **warmth of gratitude and the flow of abundance**.
2. Hold the **fossil or stone**, saying:

"From ancient Earth, from time untold,
Blessings flow, both bright and bold.
In gratitude, my heart expands,
Abundance flows from nature's hands."

1. Take the **bowl of seeds** and hold it over your heart, visualizing **gratitude growing like a great prehistoric forest**.
2. Scatter the **seeds onto the ground** (or place them in a small pouch to carry as a charm).
3. Close the ritual by saying:

"As the Earth provides, so shall I,
With open heart, let blessings fly."

◈ **Result:** This ritual **deepens gratitude, aligns your energy with abundance, and strengthens your bond with the Earth.**

10. The Ritual of Protection and Boundaries

◇ **For:** Shielding yourself with Dino Wiccan magick and setting firm personal boundaries.

Materials:

- A **black or blue candle** (for protection)
- A **stone or fossil** (preferably an armored species like Ankylosaurus or Triceratops)
- A **small bowl of salt**

◇ **Steps:**

1. Light the **black or blue candle**, visualizing **a protective shield forming around you, strong as dinosaur armor.**
2. Hold the **fossil or stone**, saying:

"Mighty beast, armored true,
Let no harm or fear pass through.
Shield me now, my space is mine,
Boundaries firm, strong as time."

1. Sprinkle **salt around your sacred space**, creating a **barrier of protection.**
2. Meditate for a few moments, **envisioning any unwanted energy bouncing off your shield.**
3. Blow out the candle, but keep the **fossil/stone as a personal protection talisman.**

◇ **Result:** This ritual **creates a strong spiritual and emotional barrier, helping you set boundaries and protect your energy.**

11. The Ritual of Cyclical Renewal
◇ **For: Releasing the old and welcoming transformation.**
Materials:

- A **small bowl of water** (symbolizing flow and change)
- A **green or white candle**
- A **leaf or feather** (representing transition)

◇ **Steps:**

1. Light the **green or white candle**, focusing on **life's endless cycles—birth, death, rebirth.**
2. Hold the **leaf or feather** and whisper into it **something you wish to release.**
3. Drop the **leaf/feather into the bowl of water**, saying:

"Like the dinosaurs who walked before,
I change, I shift, I grow once more.
Old fades away, new comes in sight,
I step ahead, my path is bright."

1. Let the **water carry away the energy of the past.** If possible, pour it onto the Earth as a sign of renewal.
2. Take a deep breath and **welcome the new cycle into your life.**

◇ **Result:** This ritual **helps with transformation, renewal, and embracing the cycles of nature.**

12. The Ritual of Love and Unity

◈ **For: Strengthening love in all its forms—self-love, friendship, romance, and universal love.**

Materials:

- A **rose quartz crystal or fossil** (symbolizing love and connection)
- A **pink, red, or white candle**
- A **cup of herbal tea or water** (for harmony)

◈ **Steps:**

1. Light the **pink/red/white candle**, visualizing **love radiating from within you.**
2. Hold the **rose quartz or fossil**, saying:

"From Earth and time, love endures,
In heart and soul, strong and pure.
Bound by trust, by kindness bright,
Love unites us, day and night."

1. Take a sip of the **tea/water**, feeling **the warmth of love spreading through your being.**
2. Hold the crystal over your heart and **send loving energy to yourself and those in your life.**
3. Close the ritual by saying:

"Love eternal, wild and free,
May its light stay strong in me."

◈ **Result:** This ritual **enhances love, unity, and strengthens connections with yourself and others.**

13. The Ritual of Legacy and Remembrance

◈ **For:** Honoring ancestors, Dino spirits, and leaving a spiritual imprint for future generations.

Materials:

- A **fossil, stone, or symbolic item**
- A **white or black candle**
- A **piece of paper and pen**

◈ **Steps:**

1. Light the **white/black candle**, honoring the **spirits of the past.**
2. Hold the **fossil or stone**, feeling the **weight of time and legacy in your hands.**
3. Write down **a message of wisdom or a lesson you wish to pass down.**
4. Read it aloud, saying:

"Ancient spirits, hear my call,
May this wisdom never fall.
Through time and stone, through land and sky,
My legacy shall never die."

1. Place the **paper under the fossil or in a sacred place**, preserving the message for the future.

◈ **Result:** This ritual **honors the past and ensures that your spiritual knowledge continues forward.**

Conclusion

These **Sacred Dino Wicca Rituals** provide a **practical way to embody the 13 principles,** strengthening your connection to prehistoric energies while honoring **Earth's cycles, transformation, and spiritual power.** May these rituals guide you **on a path of wisdom, resilience, and harmony with the ancient world.** ◈◈

Appendix C: Resources and Further Reading

Dino Wicca is a unique and evolving spiritual path that blends **prehistoric wisdom, earth-based magick, and personal transformation**. To deepen your practice, this appendix provides a **comprehensive list of resources**, including **books, websites, tools, and sacred objects** that can support your journey.

1. Essential Books on Prehistory, Spirituality, and Earth Magick

While there are no mainstream books specifically on **Dino Wicca** (yet), the following titles can help build a foundation in **prehistoric studies, animism, magick, and Earth spirituality.**

⬥ **Books on Dinosaurs and Prehistoric Life**

These books provide insight into **dinosaur behavior, ancient ecosystems, and Earth's history**, essential for connecting with the prehistoric energy in Dino Wicca.

- **The Rise and Fall of the Dinosaurs: A New History of a Lost World** – *Stephen Brusatte*
    - A detailed, up-to-date exploration of the **age of dinosaurs, their evolution, and eventual extinction.**
- **The Last Days of the Dinosaurs: An Asteroid, Extinction, and the Beginning of Our World** – *Riley Black*
    - Analyzes the world **before and after** the asteroid impact, providing a sense of **transformation and cyclical renewal.**
- **Dinosaurs Rediscovered: The Scientific Revolution in Paleontology** – *Michael J. Benton*
    - A deep dive into the **new discoveries in dinosaur science**, including behavior, social structures, and intelligence.
- **The Princeton Field Guide to Dinosaurs** – *Gregory S. Paul*
    - A **detailed illustrated reference** covering hundreds of dinosaur species.

⬥ **Books on Animism and Spiritual Connection to Ancient Earth**

These books help **deepen your connection to prehistoric spirits, Earth energies, and ancestral wisdom**.

- **Braiding Sweetgrass: Indigenous Wisdom, Scientific Knowledge, and the Teachings of Plants** – *Robin Wall Kimmerer*
    - Explores **the sacred connection between nature, history, and personal spirituality**.
- **Animism: Respecting the Living World** – *Graham Harvey*
    - Discusses the **belief that all things, including fossils and ancient landscapes, have spirit.**
- **Sacred Earth, Sacred Soul: Celtic Wisdom for Reawakening to What Our Souls Know and Healing the World** – *John Philip Newell*
    - Explores ancient **earth-based spiritual practices**, many of which can be applied to Dino Wicca.

⬥ **Books on Magick, Ritual, and Spiritual Practice**

These books will help you develop your **ritual structure, spellwork, and sacred ceremonies** in Dino Wicca.

- **The Earth Path: Grounding Your Spirit in the Rhythms of Nature** – *Starhawk*
    - Explores **nature-based spiritual practices, meditation, and honoring Earth's cycles.**
- **Walking the Tides: Seasonal Magical Rhythms and Lore** – *Nigel G. Pearson*
    - Helps align spiritual practice with the **changing seasons and natural world.**
- **Of Blood and Bones: Working with Shadow Magick & the Dark Moon** – *Kate Freuler*
    - Teaches **working with bones, fossils, and shadow work**, which align with Dino Wiccan principles.
- **The Temple of Shamanic Witchcraft: Shadows, Spirits, and the Healing Journey** – *Christopher Penczak*
    - Provides **techniques for spiritual journeying, working with ancestral spirits, and animistic practice.**

2. Websites and Online Resources

Dino Wicca is a growing practice, but many online resources can **support your understanding of prehistoric wisdom, Earth magick, and spiritual evolution.**

❖ **Websites on Dinosaurs and Prehistoric Life**

- **The Paleontology Portal** (paleoportal.org) – Offers **scientific articles, fossil databases, and prehistoric life information.**
- **The Dinosaur Database** (dinosaurpictures.org) – Explore detailed **information on various dinosaur species, including habitat and behavior.**
- **FossilEra** (fossilera.com) – A site where you can **purchase fossils for use in rituals and spiritual work.**

❖ **Websites on Animism, Earth-Based Spirituality, and Rituals**

- **Sacred Texts Archive** (sacred-texts.com) – A vast collection of **spiritual, mythological, and magical texts** that can help shape your Dino Wiccan philosophy.
- **EarthSky** (earthsky.org) – Tracks **celestial events, lunar cycles, and natural rhythms** to incorporate into your rituals.
- **The Wild Hunt** (wildhunt.org) – Covers **news, updates, and insights into modern pagan and earth-based spiritual practices.**

3. Tools for Dino Wiccan Practice

Dino Wicca blends **prehistoric energy with earth-based magick**, so the right tools can enhance your practice.

⬨ **Fossils and Sacred Objects**

- **Ammonites** – Represent **spirals of time, transformation, and deep knowledge.**
- **Trilobite Fossils** – Used for **ancestral connection and past-life exploration.**
- **Dinosaur Teeth & Claws** – Symbolize **strength, protection, and primal energy.**
- **Petrified Wood** – Helps in **grounding, stability, and connecting to prehistoric Earth.**

⬨ **Candles and Elemental Tools**

- **Green & Brown Candles** – Used for **earth-based rituals, grounding, and honoring nature.**
- **Red & Gold Candles** – Represent **strength, power, and the fire of prehistoric transformation.**
- **Volcanic Rocks & Lava Stones** – Symbolize **Earth's fiery energy and planetary shifts.**

⬨ **Journals and Books of Shadows**

- Keep a **Dino Wiccan Grimoire** to record **rituals, meditations, and personal experiences.**
- Sketch or write about **dreams involving prehistoric creatures or natural landscapes.**
- Document **fossil findings, rituals performed, and seasonal observances.**

⬨ **Divination and Meditation Tools**

- **Dinomancy (Divination with Fossils)** – Hold a fossil and meditate, asking for insights.
- **Tarot & Oracle Decks (Nature-Based)** – Use cards related to **Earth magick, animal spirits, or prehistoric themes.**
- **Pendulums (Made of Fossil Stone)** – Used to seek guidance from **dinosaur spirits and Earth energies.**

4. Podcasts, YouTube Channels, and Documentaries
◈ **Podcasts for Spiritual and Prehistoric Wisdom**

- **Earth Ancients Podcast** – Explores **lost civilizations, ancient Earth, and spiritual history.**
- **Palaeocast** – Covers **fossil discoveries and the prehistoric world.**

◈ **YouTube Channels for Dino Wicca Inspiration**

- **PBS Eons** – Covers **prehistoric life and evolution.**
- **The Wild Witch** – Focuses on **earth-based and animistic spirituality.**
- **New Earth Ancient Knowledge** – Explores **spirituality, natural cycles, and sacred sites.**

◈ **Documentaries to Deepen Your Connection**

- **Prehistoric Planet (Apple TV+)** – A highly detailed documentary on dinosaur life.
- **Walking with Dinosaurs (BBC)** – Classic series exploring dinosaurs in their natural environments.
- **The Universe: Ancient Earth (Netflix)** – Examines the Earth's evolution, including prehistoric life.

Conclusion: Expanding Your Dino Wicca Journey

These **books, websites, tools, and media resources** will support you as you walk the **Dino Wiccan path**, deepening your understanding of **prehistoric energy, spiritual transformation, and Earth-based wisdom.**

Remember: Dino Wicca is a **living, evolving path**—just like the great creatures of the past, you are constantly **growing, adapting, and discovering new layers of ancient truth.** ◈◈

May these resources **guide you in wisdom, strength, and connection to the eternal cycles of life!**

Appendix D: Dino Spirit Profiles
Detailed Descriptions of Key Dinosaur Spirits and Their Spiritual Significance

In **Dino Wicca**, the spirits of dinosaurs **serve as guides, protectors, and teachers**, each carrying distinct energies that align with **specific magickal practices and spiritual growth.** By working with **Dino Spirits**, practitioners can tap into **ancient wisdom, primal power, and natural cycles** that transcend time.

This appendix explores **key dinosaur spirits**, their **symbolism, spiritual attributes, and how to work with them** in your practice.

◈ Tyrannosaurus Rex – The Spirit of Power and Leadership
Spiritual Meaning:

The **T. rex spirit** embodies **dominance, confidence, and the ability to stand your ground.** It is a symbol of **strength, fearlessness, and reclaiming personal power.**

Attributes & Magickal Associations:

- **Confidence & Personal Strength** – Helps in overcoming fear and self-doubt.
- **Leadership & Commanding Presence** – Assists those stepping into **authority roles** or needing to assert themselves.
- **Survival & Tenacity** – Teaches resilience in the face of challenges.
- **Warrior Spirit** – Can be invoked in protection magick and defensive spellwork.

How to Work with T. rex Energy:

◈ **Wear a fossilized T. rex tooth or a replica** to invoke its **protective and dominant energy.**
◈ **Use red, gold, and black candles** in rituals for **strength and courage.**
◈ **Stand in a power stance and visualize a T. rex walking beside you** when preparing for challenges.
◈ **T. rex Affirmation:**

"I stand strong, unshaken, and fearless. I command my space with power and confidence."

◈ **Brachiosaurus – The Spirit of Growth and Wisdom**
Spiritual Meaning:
The **Brachiosaurus spirit** represents **patience, higher knowledge, and long-term vision.** It is a symbol of **gentle strength and wisdom gained through experience.**
Attributes & Magickal Associations:

- **Growth & Stability** – Encourages slow, steady progress.
- **Higher Knowledge & Spiritual Awareness** – Assists in deepening **intuition and wisdom.**
- **Endurance & Longevity** – Helps in **persevering through life's challenges.**
- **Peaceful Strength** – Promotes **calm resilience over aggression.**

How to Work with Brachiosaurus Energy:
◈ **Meditate under a large tree**, envisioning its wisdom flowing into you.
◈ **Use green and brown candles** in rituals for **stability and learning.**
◈ **Place a fossilized leaf or petrified wood on your altar** to connect with Brachiosaurus energy.
◈ **Brachiosaurus Affirmation:**
"I grow strong and wise, embracing the lessons of time and patience."

◈ **Triceratops – The Spirit of Protection and Boundaries**
Spiritual Meaning:
The **Triceratops spirit** teaches the **importance of setting boundaries, protecting oneself, and standing firm against external pressures.** It is a guardian spirit for those who need **emotional, physical, or energetic protection.**
Attributes & Magickal Associations:

- **Boundary Setting & Self-Defense** – Helps create **emotional shields against negativity.**
- **Loyalty & Family Protection** – Aids in strengthening bonds and **protecting loved ones.**
- **Grounding & Stability** – Helps in **staying centered in times of uncertainty.**

How to Work with Triceratops Energy:
◈ **Carry a piece of hematite, tiger's eye, or black tourmaline** for protection.
◈ **Visualize a Triceratops creating a protective barrier around you.**
◈ **Use a circle of salt or stones** in protection rituals.
◈ **Triceratops Affirmation:**
"I protect my space, my energy, and my boundaries with strength and honor."

◈ **Pteranodon – The Spirit of Freedom and Higher Vision**
Spiritual Meaning:
The **Pteranodon spirit** represents **expansion, freedom, and seeing beyond limitations.** It helps with **mental clarity, insight, and breaking free from restrictions.**
Attributes & Magickal Associations:

- Higher Perspective & Intuition – Assists in **making wise decisions.**
- Breaking Free from Limitations – Encourages **boldness and independence.**
- Mental Clarity & Vision – Helps in **planning for the future.**
- Air Element & Travel Magick – Can be invoked for **safe journeys and new experiences.**

How to Work with Pteranodon Energy:
◈ **Meditate while looking at the sky,** asking for guidance on **seeing the bigger picture.**
◈ **Use feathers, clear quartz, or blue candles** in rituals for **mental clarity.**
◈ **Call upon Pteranodon before making major life decisions.**
◈ **Pteranodon Affirmation:**
"I soar above limitations, seeing the vast possibilities before me."

◈ **Velociraptor – The Spirit of Strategy and Quick Thinking**
Spiritual Meaning:
The **Velociraptor spirit** is associated with **agility, intelligence, and adaptability.** It is an excellent guide for problem-solving and quick decision-making.
Attributes & Magickal Associations:

- **Speed & Adaptability** – Helps in **quickly adjusting to new situations.**
- **Strategic Thinking** – Strengthens **logic, planning, and execution.**
- **Mental Agility & Cunning** – Aids in **outmaneuvering obstacles and challenges.**

How to Work with Velociraptor Energy:
◈ **Use yellow and silver candles** to enhance **mental focus.**
◈ **Wear a small fossil or talisman** when needing **quick wit and cleverness.**
◈ **Call on Velociraptor energy before tests, interviews, or competitions.**
◈ **Velociraptor Affirmation:**
"I move swiftly and think clearly, navigating all challenges with ease."

◈ **Ankylosaurus – The Spirit of Defense and Strength**
Spiritual Meaning:
The **Ankylosaurus spirit** represents **protection, resilience, and self-preservation.** It is a powerful **guardian against negativity, psychic attacks, and harmful influences.**
Attributes & Magickal Associations:

- **Defensive Energy & Warding** – Creates a **shield of protection around the practitioner.**
- **Emotional Resilience** – Helps in **staying strong through difficulties.**
- **Fortified Boundaries** – Prevents **toxic energy from entering one's life.**

How to Work with Ankylosaurus Energy:
◈ **Create a protective sigil using fossil symbols.**
◈ **Wear obsidian or onyx** for spiritual shielding.
◈ **Visualize an Ankylosaurus tail swinging behind you, clearing away threats.**
◈ **Ankylosaurus Affirmation:**
"I am strong, unbreakable, and protected in all that I do."

Conclusion: Connecting with Dino Spirits
Dino spirits **offer guidance, protection, and wisdom,** aligning their **unique strengths with our personal journeys.** By honoring their energy, we **awaken the prehistoric power that still flows through the Earth.**
◈ **How to Deepen Your Connection:**

- **Meditate with fossils or dinosaur imagery.**
- **Keep a journal of dreams or signs involving dinosaurs.**
- **Create an altar dedicated to your chosen Dino spirit.**

May the wisdom of the **prehistoric world** guide you on your path, helping you walk with **strength, knowledge, and harmony with ancient energies.** ◈◈

Message from the Author:

I hope you enjoyed this book, I love astrology and knew there was not a book such as this out on the shelf. I love metaphysical items as well. Please check out my other books:

-Life of Government Benefits

-My life of Hell

-My life with Hydrocephalus

-Red Sky

-World Domination:Woman's rule

-World Domination:Woman's Rule 2: The War

-Life and Banishment of Apophis: book 1

-The Kidney Friendly Diet

-The Ultimate Hemp Cookbook

-Creating a Dispensary(legally)

-Cleanliness throughout life: the importance of showering from childhood to adulthood.

-Strong Roots: The Risks of Overcoddling children

-Hemp Horoscopes: Cosmic Insights and Earthly Healing

- Celestial Hemp Navigating the Zodiac: Through the Green Cosmos

-Astrological Hemp: Aligning The Stars with Earth's Ancient Herb

-The Astrological Guide to Hemp: Stars, Signs, and Sacred Leaves

-Green Growth: Innovative Marketing Strategies for your Hemp Products and Dispensary

-Cosmic Cannabis

-Astrological Munchies

-Henry The Hemp

-Zodiacal Roots: The Astrological Soul Of Hemp

- **Green Constellations: Intersection of Hemp and Zodiac**

-Hemp in The Houses: An astrological Adventure Through The Cannabis Galaxy

-Galactic Ganja Guide

Heavenly Hemp

Zodiac Leaves

Doctor Who Astrology

Cannastrology

Stellar Satvias and Cosmic Indicas

Celestial Cannabis: A Zodiac Journey

AstroHerbology: The Sky and The Soil: Volume 1
AstroHerbology:Celestial Cannabis:Volume 2
Cosmic Cannabis Cultivation
The Starry Guide to Herbal Harmony: Volume 1
The Starry Guide to Herbal Harmony: Cannabis Universe: Volume 2
Yugioh Astrology: Astrological Guide to Deck, Duels and more
Nightmare Mansion: Echoes of The Abyss
Nightmare Mansion 2: Legacy of Shadows
Nightmare Mansion 3: Shadows of the Forgotten
Nightmare Mansion 4: Echoes of the Damned
The Life and Banishment of Apophis: Book 2
Nightmare Mansion: Halls of Despair
<u>Healing with Herb: Cannabis and Hydrocephalus</u>
<u>Planetary Pot: Aligning with Astrological Herbs: Volume 1</u>
Fast Track to Freedom: 30 Days to Financial Independence Using AI, Assets, and Agile Hustles
<u>Cosmic Hemp Pathways</u>
How to Become Financially Free in 30 Days: 10,000 Paths to Prosperity
Zodiacal Herbage: Astrological Insights: Volume 1
Nightmare Mansion: Whispers in the Walls
The Daleks Invade Atlantis
Henry the hemp and Hydrocephalus

10X The Kidney Friendly Diet
Cannabis Universe: Adult coloring book
Hemp Astrology: The Healing Power of the Stars
Zodiacal Herbage: Astrological Insights: Cannabis Universe: Volume 2
<u>Planetary Pot: Aligning with Astrological Herbs: Cannabis Universes: Volume 2</u>
Doctor Who Meets the Replicators and SG-1: The Ultimate Battle for Survival
Nightmare Mansion: Curse of the Blood Moon
<u>The Celestial Stoner: A Guide to the Zodiac</u>
Cosmic Pleasures: Sex Toy Astrology for Every Sign
Hydrocephalus Astrology: Navigating the Stars and Healing Waters
Lapis and the Mischievous Chocolate Bar

Celestial Positions: Sexual Astrology for Every Sign
Apophis's Shadow Work Journal: : A Journey of Self-Discovery and Healing
Kinky Cosmos: Sexual Kink Astrology for Every Sign
Digital Cosmos: The Astrological Digimon Compendium
Stellar Seeds: The Cosmic Guide to Growing with Astrology
Apophis's Daily Gratitude Journal

Cat Astrology: Feline Mysteries of the Cosmos
The Cosmic Kama Sutra: An Astrological Guide to Sexual Positions
Unleash Your Potential: A Guided Journal Powered by AI Insights
Whispers of the Enchanted Grove

Cosmic Pleasures: An Astrological Guide to Sexual Kinks
369, 12 Manifestation Journal
Whisper of the nocturne journal(blank journal for writing or drawing)
The Boogey Book
Locked In Reflection: A Chastity Journey Through Locktober
Generating Wealth Quickly:
How to Generate $100,000 in 24 Hours
Star Magic: Harness the Power of the Universe
The Flatulence Chronicles: A Fart Journal for Self-Discovery
The Doctor and The Death Moth
Seize the Day: A Personal Seizure Tracking Journal
The Ultimate Boogeyman Safari: A Journey into the Boogie World and Beyond
Whispers of Samhain: 1,000 Spells of Love, Luck, and Lunar Magic: Samhain Spell Book
Apophis's guides:
Witch's Spellbook Crafting Guide for Halloween
<u>**Frost & Flame: The Enchanted Yule Grimoire of 1000 Winter Spells**</u>
<u>**The Ultimate Boogey Goo Guide & Spooky Activities for Halloween Fun**</u>
Harmony of the Scales: A Libra's Spellcraft for Balance and Beauty
The Enchanted Advent: 36 Days of Christmas Wonders

Nightmare Mansion: The Labyrinth of Screams
Harvest of Enchantment: 1,000 Spells of Gratitude, Love, and Fortune for Thanksgiving
The Boogey Chronicles: A Journal of Nightly Encounters and Shadowy Secrets
The 12 Days of Financial Freedom: A Step-by-Step Christmas Countdown to Transform Your Finances
Sigil of the Eternal Spiral Blank Journal
A Christmas Feast: Timeless Recipes for Every Meal
Holiday Stress-Free Solutions: A Survival Guide to Thriving During the Festive Season
Yu-Gi-Oh! Holiday Gifting Mastery: The Ultimate Guide for Fans and Newcomers Alike
Holiday Harmony: A Hydrocephalus Survival Guide for the Festive Season
Celestial Craft: The Witch's Almanac for 2025 – A Cosmic Guide to Manifestations, Moons, and Mystical Events
Doctor Who: The Toymaker's Winter Wonderland
Tulsa King Unveiled: A Thrilling Guide to Stallone's Mafia Masterpiece
Pendulum Craft: A Complete Guide to Crafting and Using Personalized Divination Tools
Nightmare Mansion: Santa's Eternal Eve

Starlight Noel: A Cosmic Journey through Christmas Mysteries
The Dark Architect: Unlocking the Blueprint of Existence
Surviving the Embrace: The Ultimate Guide to Encounters with The Hugging Molly
The Enchanted Codex: Secrets of the Craft for Witches, Wiccans, and Pagans
Harvest of Gratitude: A Complete Thanksgiving Guide
Yuletide Essentials: A Complete Guide to an Authentic and Magical Christmas
Celestial Smokes: A Cosmic Guide to Cigars and Astrology
Living in Balance: A Comprehensive Survival Guide to Thriving with Diabetes Insipidus
Cosmic Symbiosis: The Venom Zodiac Chronicles

The Cursed Paw of Ambition

Cosmic Symbiosis: The Astrological Venom Journal
Celestial Wonders Unfold: A Stargazer's Guide to the Cosmos (2024-2029)
The Ultimate Black Friday Prepper's Guide: Mastering Shopping Strategies and Savings

Cosmic Sales: The Astrological Guide to Black Friday Shopping

Legends of the Corn Mother and Other Harvest Myths
Whispers of the Harvest: The Corn Mother's Journal
The Evergreen Spellbook
The Doctor Meets the Boogeyman
The White Witch of Rose Hall's SpellBook

The Gingerbread Golem's Shadow: A Study in Sweet Darkness

The Gingerbread Golem Codex: An Academic Exploration of Sweet Myths

The Gingerbread Golem Grimoire: Sweet Magicks and Spells for the Festive Witch

The Curse of the Gingerbread Golem

10-minute Christmas Crafts for kids

<u>Christmas Crisis Solutions: The Ultimate Last-Minute Survival Guide</u>

Gingerbread Golem Recipes: Holiday Treats with a Magical Twist

The Infinite Key: Unlocking Mystical Secrets of the Ages

Enchanted Yule: A Wiccan and Pagan Guide to a Magical and Memorable Season
Dinosaurs of Power: Unlocking Ancient Magick
Astro-Dinos: The Cosmic Guide to Prehistoric Wisdom
Gallifrey's Yule Logs: A Festive Doctor Who Cookbook

The Dino Grimoire: Secrets of Prehistoric Magick

The Gift They Never Knew They Needed

The Gingerbread Golem's Culinary Alchemy: Enchanting Recipes for a Sweetly Dark Feast

A Time Lord Christmas: Holiday Adventures with the Doctor

Krampusproofing Your Home: Defensive Strategies for Yule

Silent Frights: A Collection of Christmas Creepypastas to Chill Your Bones

Santa Raptor's Jolly Carnage: A Dino-Claus Christmas Tale

Prehistoric Palettes: A Dino Wicca Coloring Journey
The Christmas Wishkeeper Chronicles
The Starlight Sleigh: A Holiday Journey

Elf Secrets: The True Magic of the North Pole
Candy Cane Conjurations
Cooking with Kids: Recipes Under 20 Minutes
Doctor Who: The TARDIS Confiscation
The Anxiety First Aid Kit: Quick Tools to Calm Your Mind
Frosty Whispers: A Winter's Tale
The Infinite Key: Unlocking the Secrets to Prosperity, Resilience, and Purpose
The Grasping Void: Why You'll Regret This Purchase
Astrology for Busy Bees: Star Signs Simplified
The Instant Focus Formula: Cut Through the Noise
The Secret Language of Colors: Unlocking the Emotional Codes
Sacred Fossil Chronicles: Blank Journal
The Christmas Cottage Miracle
Feeding Frenzy: Graboid-Inspired Recipes
Manifest in Minutes: The Quick Law of Attraction Guide
The Symbiote Chronicles: Doctor Who's Venomous Journey
Think Tiny, Grow Big: The Minimalist Mindset
The Energy Key: Unlocking Limitless Motivation
New Year, New Magic: Manifesting Your Best Year Yet
Unstoppable You: Mastering Confidence in Minutes
Infinite Energy: The Secret to Never Feeling Drained
Lightning Focus: Mastering the Art of Productivity in a Distracted World
Saturnalia Manifestation Magick: A Guide to Unlocking Abundance During the Solstice
Graboids and Garland: The Ultimate Tremors-Themed Christmas Guide
12 Nights of Holiday Magic
The Power of Pause: 60-Second Mindfulness Practices
The Quick Reset: How to Reclaim Your Life After Burnout
The Shadow Eater: A Tale of Despair and Survival
The Micro-Mastery Method: Transform Your Skills in Just Minutes a Day
Reclaiming Time: How to Live More by Doing Less
Chronovore: The Eternal Nexus
The Mind Reset: Unlocking Your Inner Peace in a Chaotic World
Confidence Code: Building Unshakable Self-Belief
Baby the Vampire Terrier
Baby the Vampire Terrier's Christmas Adventure
Celestial Streams: The Content Creator's Astrology Manual
The Wealth Whisperer: Unlocking Abundance with Everyday Actions
The Energy Equation: Maximize Your Output Without Burning Out
The Happiness Algorithm: Science-Backed Steps to Joyful Living
Stress-Free Success: Achieving Goals Without Anxiety
Mindful Wealth: The New Blueprint for Financial Freedom

The Festive Flavors of New Year: A Culinary Celebration
The Master's Gambit: Keys of Eternal Power
Shadowed Secrets: Groundhog Day Mysteries
Beneath the Burrow: Lessons from the Groundhog
Spring's Whispers: The Groundhog's Prediction
The Limitless Mindset: Unlock Your Untapped Potential
The Focus Funnel: How to Cut Through Chaos and Get Results
Bold Moves: Building Courage to Live on Your Terms
The Daily Shift: Simple Practices for Lasting Transformation
The Quarter-Life Reset: Thriving in Your 20s and 30s
The Art of Shadowplay: Building Your Own Personal Myth
The Eternal Loop: Finding Purpose in Repetition
Burrowing Wisdom: Life Lessons from the Groundhog
Shadow Work: A Groundhog Day Perspective
Love in Bloom: 5-Minute Romantic Gestures
The Shadowspell Codex: Secrets of Forbidden Magick
The Burnout Cure: Finding Balance in a Busy World
The Groundhog Prophecy: Unlocking Seasonal Secrets
Nog Tales: The Spirited History of Eggnog
Six More Weeks: Embracing Seasonal Transitions
The Lumivian Chronicles: Fragments of the Fifth Dimension
Money on Your Mind: A Beginner's Guide to Wealth
The Focus Fix: Breaking Through Distraction
January's Spirit Keepers: Mystical Protectors of the Cold
Creativity Unchained: Unlocking Your Wildest Ideas in 2025
Manifestation Mastery: 365 Days to Rewrite Your Reality
The Groundhog's Mirror: Reflecting on Change
The Weeping Angels' Christmas Curse
Burrowed in Time: A Groundhog Day Journey
Heartbeats: Poems to Share with Your Valentine
Dino Wicca: The Sacred Grimoire of Prehistoric Magick
Courage of the Pride: Finding Your Inner Roar
The Lion's Leap: Bold Moves for Big Results
Healthy Hustle: Achieving Without Overworking
Practical Manifesting: Turning Dreams into Reality in 2025
Jurassic Pharaohs: Unlocking the Magick of Ancient Egypt and Dino Wicca
The Happiness Equation: Small Changes for Big Joy
The Confidence Compass: Finding Your Inner Strength
Whispers in the Hollow: Tales of the Forgotten Beasts
Echoes from the Hollow: The Return of Forgotten Beasts
The Hollow Ascendant: The Rise of the Forgotten Beasts

The Relationship Reset: Building Better Connections
Mastering the Morning: How to Win the Day Before 8 AM
The Shadow's Dance: Groundhog Day Symbolism
Cupid's Kitchen: Quick Valentine's Day Recipes
Valentine's Day on a Budget: Love Without Breaking the Bank
Astrocraft: Aligning the Stars in the World of Minecraft
Forecasting Life: Groundhog Day Reflections
Bleeding Hearts: Twisted Tales of Valentine's Terror
Herbal Smoke Revolution: The Ultimate Guide to Nature's Cigarette Alternative
Winter's Wrath: The Complete Survival Blueprint for Extreme Freezes.
The Groundhog's Shadow: A Tale of Seasons
Burrowed Insights: Wisdom from the Groundhog
Sensual Strings: The Art of Erotic Bondage
Whispered Flames: Unlocking the Power of Fire Play
Forgotten Shadows: A Guide to Cryptids Lost to Time
Six Weeks of Secrets: Groundhog Day's Hidden Messages
Shadows and Cycles: Groundhog Day Reflections
The Art of Love Letters: Crafting the Perfect Message
Romantic Getaways at Home: Turning Your Space into Paradise
Purrfect Brews: A Cat Lover's Guide to Coffee and Companionship
The Groundhog's Wisdom: Timeless Lessons for Modern Life
The Shadow Oracle: Groundhog Day as a Predictor
Emerging from the Burrow: A Journey of Renewal
The Language of Love: Learning Your Partner's Love Style
Authorpreneur: The Ultimate Blueprint for Writing, Publishing, and Thriving as an Author
Weathering the Seasons: Groundhog Day Perspectives
Valentine's Day Magic: A Guide to Romantic Rituals
The Shadow Chronicles: Stories of Groundhog Day
Love and Laughter: Fun Games for Valentine's Day
AstroRealty: Unlocking the Stars for Property Success
The Groundhog's Path: A Guide to Seasonal Balance
Groundhog Day Diaries: Reflections in the Shadow
The Groundhog's Light: Illuminating the Path Ahead
Valentine's Traditions from Around the World
AI Wealth Revolution: Unlocking the Trillionaire Mindset
Love Rekindled: Reigniting Passion in Relationships
Single and Thriving: Self-Love on Valentine's Day
Emerald Legends: Mystical Tales of Ireland
Green Alchemy: Harnessing Nature's Magic
The Hearts of Horror: A Valentine's Day Nightmare

The Leprechaun's Guide to Wealth and Wisdom
Dancing with the Sidhe: Celebrating the Otherworld
Shamrocks and Shadows: Mysteries of the Green Isle
Emerald Energy: Harnessing Luck and Growth
The Gingerbread Golem's Valentine: A Sweetheart's Guide to Love and Enchantment
The Celtic Knot: Weaving Life and Destiny
Green Fire: Elemental Magic for St. Patrick's Day
Clover Chronicles: Finding Your Inner Luck
Ireland's Mystical Creatures: A Field Guide
Gingerbread Golem's Love Almanac
Prowl and Thrive: The Lion's Guide to Success
Love Alchemy: Transforming Your Life Through Heart Energy
WORLD DOMINATION: Woman's Rule 3:
The New Life
The Midnight Rose: A Guide to Lunar Love Spells
The Forbidden Letters: Writing Your Own Love Prophecy
Luck and Lore: St. Patrick's Day for Modern Mystics
The Green Path: A Pagan Celebration of Renewal
The Dark Architect's Guide to Reprogramming Reality
Unlocking the Hidden Layers of Creation
Prankster's Paradise: A Guide to Harmless Hijinks
Manifest Your Reality: The Law of Attraction Simplified
The TARDIS Owner's Manual: Understanding the Doctor's Ship: *A complete guide to the TARDIS, its technology, secrets, and mysteries*
Starlit Romance: Astrology Secrets for Finding True Love
The Time Lord's Atlas: A Complete Guide to the Whoniverse: *A breakdown of the locations, planets, and dimensions explored in Doctor Who*
Sweetheart Shadows: The Dark Side of Love and Attraction
February Fire: Reigniting Passion in Every Area of Life
The Self-Love Toolkit: 5 Ways to Embrace Who You Are
February Sparks: Ignite Your Dreams in 28 Days
March to Success: A 31-Day Action Blueprint

If you want solar for your home go here: https://www.harborsolar.live/apophisenterprises/

Get Some Tarot cards: https://www.makeplayingcards.com/sell/apophis-occult-shop

Get some shirts: https://www.bonfire.com/store/apophis-shirt-emporium/

Instagrams:
@apophis_enterprises,
@apophisbookemporium,
@apophisscardshop
Twitter: @apophisenterpr1
Tiktok:@apophisenterprise
Youtube: @sg1fan23477, @FiresideRetreatKingdom
Hive: @sg1fan23477
CheeLee: @SG1fan23477

Podcast: Apophis Chat Zone: https://open.spotify.com/show/5zXbr-CLEV2xzCp8ybrfHsk?si=fb4d4fdbdce44dec

Newsletter: https://apophiss-newsletter-27c897.beehiiv.com/

If you want to support me or see posts of other projects that I have come over to: **buymeacoffee.com/mpetchinskg**

I post there daily several times a day

Get your Dinowicca or Christmas themed digital products, especially Santa Raptor songs and other musics. Here: **https://sg1fan23477.gumroad.com**

Apophis Yuletide Digital has not only digital Christmas items, but it will have all things with Dinowicca as well as other Digital products.